Frederic William Levander

Questions on the English Language

set at the matriculation examinations of the University of London, 1858-1889

Frederic William Levander

Questions on the English Language
set at the matriculation examinations of the University of London, 1858-1889

ISBN/EAN: 9783337429102

Printed in Europe, USA, Canada, Australia, Japan

Cover: Foto ©Suzi / pixelio.de

More available books at **www.hansebooks.com**

QUESTIONS

ON THE

ENGLISH LANGUAGE

SET AT THE

MATRICULATION EXAMINATIONS

OF THE

UNIVERSITY OF LONDON, 1858–1889.

COLLECTED AND ARRANGED BY

F. W. LEVANDER, F.R.A.S.

ASSISTANT MASTER, UNIVERSITY COLLEGE SCHOOL, LONDON;
AUTHOR OF "SOLUTIONS OF QUESTIONS ON MAGNETISM AND ELECTRICITY,"
"TEST QUESTIONS ON THE LATIN LANGUAGE," "A GENERAL INDEX
TO THE ASTRONOMICAL REGISTER," AND EDITOR OF
"MATRICULATION QUESTIONS ON HISTORY
AND GEOGRAPHY"

SECOND EDITION, WITH APPENDICES

LONDON

H. K. LEWIS, 136, GOWER STREET

1889

PREFATORY NOTE.

In the present Edition the Questions have been brought up to date, and include those set at the Matriculation Examination held in the present month. In order to render the book more useful, I have added some Hints to Candidates, as well as various Tables in connection with the subject. For the latter I gratefully acknowledge my indebtedness to Fleming's "Analysis of the English Language," and to Dr. Morris' "Historical English Grammar"; and, for general assistance, to the Notes used for the preparation of Candidates for Matriculation by W. STAINTON-MOSES, M.A., Chief of the English Department in University College School.

January, 1889.

029

CONTENTS.

———•◦•———

QUESTIONS ON THE ENGLISH LANGUAGE.

—◆◆—

I. HISTORY OF THE LANGUAGE AND OF THE ARYAN FAMILY OF LANGUAGES.

(MORRIS, Chaps. 1-3).

1. To what family of Languages does English belong? Give any facts showing its relation to some other languages of Europe. (1879).

2. Represent in tabular form the stocks and languages of the Indo-European family that have contributed to the formation of English. (1883).

3. Show the relation between English and the other languages of the Indo-European Family. (1881).

4. Sketch the position of English among allied languages. (1879).

5. Make a table showing the relationship of English to the other languages of the Indo-European Family. (1873, 1880).

6. Express, in a tabular form, the relationship of English to other Teutonic languages. (1888).

7. Both from its vocabulary and its grammar, as they now are, show that English is a Teutonic language. (1887).

8. Show clearly that English in its origin and

B

basis is a Teutonic language. Also say by what
Teutonic languages it has been affected and
influenced since its coming into this island.
(1886).

9. In what parts of speech, and in what classes
of terms, have we the greatest proportion of words
of Saxon origin? Give examples of any words
which you know by their form or spelling to be of
foreign derivation. (1863).

10. What traces in particular have Danish Invasions left in the language of this country? (1877).

11. Point out some of the chief signs of Teutonic
origin in English words. (1872).

12. In what directions and through what channels
has the Latin language left its impress on English?
(1885).

13. Mention the various times and ways in which
Latin, directly or indirectly, has increased our
vocabulary. (1886).

14. In what way, and at what times, have Latin
elements been introduced into the English language?
(1877).

15. Mention some ten Latin words that appear
in English in two forms, one coming directly, the
other indirectly. (1884).

16. At what different periods has a Latin element
been introduced into our language? Give examples
of Latin words introduced in the several periods
mentioned. (1831).

17. Account historically for the presence in our
language of so many words of Latin origin.
Under what circumstances have the most important
additions of this kind been made? and what is the
neral character of words so derived? (1861).

18. Enumerate the channels through which
words from the Latin were introduced into English,
and classify the Latin elements accordingly. (1876).

19. Distinguish the successive periods of the introduction of a Latin element into English, and illustrate by examples the effect of each upon the language. (1882).

20. Distinguish between the Classical and the Teutonic elements in English. Point out the several ways in which words of Latin origin have been introduced into the language. (1880).

21. With what languages of Europe is English in origin most closely connected? What exactly is its relation to Latin? What to French? (1883).

22. At what time, and through what channels, have Classical and Romance words come into the English language? (1888).

23. Show as definitely as you can the influence of Norman-French upon our grammar. (1884).

24. Illustrate the influence which the Classical element has had upon modern English, directly and through the medium of the Romance languages. (1888).

25. Take the following sentence, and arrange in three groups the words of Saxon, Greek, and Latin origin respectively; give fully the derivation of the words italicised :—

> " Not *second* he, who rode *sublime*
> Upon the *seraph* wings of *ecstacy*
> The *secret* of the abyss to spy.
> He passed the flaming bounds of place and time,
> The living throne, the sapphire blaze,
> Where angels tremble while they gaze,
> He saw ; but, blasted with excess of light,
> Closed his eyes in endless night." (1869).

26. Distinguish between the words of Classical and Teutonic origin in the following sentences :—

"Thus it appears necessary that a man should be a nice critic in his mother-tongue before he attempts to translate in a foreign language. Neither

B 2

ENGLISH LANGUAGE.

4

is it enough that he be able to judge of words and style, but he must be a master of them too : he must perfectly understand his author's tongue, and absolutely command his own; so that to be a thorough translator he must be a thorough poet." (1888).

27. Show, by six instances of each kind, how some words have come to us directly from Latin, and some through the medium of the Romance languages. (1889).

28. Give six examples of words of Greek, Latin, and Saxon origin respectively; and state how from each word itself, its form or spelling or affixes, you tell its origin. (1863).

29. What foreign ingredients are to be found in our English vocabulary? Account historically for their presence. (1872).

30. Write down the words in the Lord's prayer which are not of Saxon origin. (1866).

31. Explain the term Anglo-Saxon. What objections are there to it? What terms have been proposed in its stead? Give reason for its retention. (1883).

32. Give, as concisely as you can, equivalents of Saxon origin for the following words:—*frustrate, eliminate, elucidate, desiderate, prevaricate, identical, eradicate, corroborate, reciprocal, internecine.* (1889).

33. Point out the advantages and disadvantages of a mixed vocabulary. How is it that ours is so mixed as it is? (1884).

34. Give a pedigree of the English language which shall show from what sources it has been successively enriched. Give dates. (1876).

35. How far back can the English language be traced by written remains? State how it may be divided into *periods* (with dates), and give the distinguishing features of each period. (1878).

36. Into what Periods may the language of this country be conveniently divided? Indicate briefly the grammatical characteristics of each. (1877).

37. Name the main sources which have contributed to form modern English, and state the period at which the influence of each has been chiefly felt. (1885).

38. What are the principal epochs and events which mark the growth of the language of this country? (1876).

39. Chaucer has been called "the well of English undefiled." Discuss this with reference to the growth of English in Chaucer's time. (1888).

40. State some differences as regards verbal forms, case-endings and suffixes, between the English of the 14th century and that of the present day. (1888).

41. Explain and illustrate the terms Synthetic and Analytic as applied to Languages. By which would you describe the English language as it now is? (1887).

42. In what classes of terms, and among what parts of speech, do we find the largest proportion of purely English words? How do you account for the presence in our vocabulary of so many words of foreign origin? (1870).

43. Discuss the use and abuse of technical terms. Whence do we chiefly obtain them? (1888).

44. From what sources do we principally obtain our naval, agricultural, and political terms? Illustrate your answers by instances. (1889).

45. Explain, by reference to the history of the language, the difference between the past tenses and participles of the following verbs:—*say, think, give, sleep, wake, run, bid, fly.* (1873).

46. Give as many examples as you can, and as the time allows, of the way in which the study of the

English Language illustrates and corroborates what
we learn from English History. (1877).

47. Give an estimate of the number of words in
our language, and of the proportion of them of
native and of foreign growth respectively. Show
when, and in what way, the greater part of such
exotic words has been introduced into our vocabulary. (1871).

48. What are the two main sources from which
the English Vocabulary is derived? From which
of them comes our Grammar? Illustrate your
answers by examples. (1885).

49. Distinguish between the Teutonic and
Romance elements of the English Vocabulary; and
write two short sentences, one containing no words
of Romance origin, the other none of Teutonic.
Which is the easier sentence to write, and why?
(1887).

50. Rewrite the following passage, by substituting
words of Saxon origin for those of Greek or Latin
origin:—

"The old man trusts wholly to slow contrivance
and gradual progression. The youth expects to
force his way by genius, vigour, and precipitance.
The old man deifies prudence. The youth commits
himself to magnanimity and chance. Age looks
with anger on the temerity of youth, and youth
with contempt on the scrupulosity of age." (*Dr.
Johnson*). (1875).

51. From what languages, and at what dates,
have we received the following words?—*Orange*;
Receive; *Street*; *Bosh*; *Boom*; *Chintz*; *Kiln*;
Fetish; *Die*; *Armadillo*; *Concatenation*; *Chess*;
Chagrin; *Pool*; *Carouse*. (1879).

52. Explain exactly the following, commenting
upon anything which is archaic in usage:—

(a) Truly and indifferently to minister justice.
(b) Let him pursue his course without let or
hindrance.
(c) Prevent us in all our doings.
(d) In good sooth.
(e) Vouchsafe us thy help.   (1889).

53. Several words are found to be common to the
dialect of Scott and that of Chaucer.   Can you account for this?   (1888).

54. Mention as many words as you can that have
been adopted into our language during the last half
century.   (1887).

II. Phonology—Grimm's Law.

Morris, Chaps. 4, 5).

55. Define the terms *letter, mute, vowel, spirant, palatal*. (1884).

56. Define the terms *vowel, diphthong, consonant*. (1880).

57. Explain all terms used in the classification of the Letters of the Alphabet. (1874).

58. What is meant by the "organs of speech"? (1886).

59. Tell what you know of the origin and structure of the English Alphabet. (1883, 1886).

60. Indicate some of the most important facts in the history of our Alphabet, and account, as far as you can, for the order in which its letters follow one another. (1880).

61. What is the use of an Alphabet? Give some account of our Alphabet, with reference both to its origin and to the classification of its letters. (1875).

62. What is meant by a "letter"? (1885).

63. Classify the letters of the Alphabet according to their sounds. (1879).

64. Classify the letters of the English Alphabet according to the parts of the vocal organs pronouncing them. (1888).

65. Give some account of our Alphabet, with reference both to its history and to the classification of the sounds it represents. (1873).

66. How would you define a "vowel"? How a "diphthong"? (1886).

67. What Vowel-sounds exist in English ? Show particularly how they are all expressed by means of the six Roman Vowels. (1879).

68. How many Vowel-sounds are there in English ? How are they represented in the written language ? Write down a word illustrating each of them. (1868).

69. How many more Vowel-sounds has English than Vowels? (1886).

70. How many Vowel *Sounds* are there in the English language ? Make a list of them, showing by how many modes of spelling each may be represented, and giving in every case a *word* containing the sound which you wish to distinguish. (1864).

71. How many Vowel-sounds are used in speaking English ? Which are they ? How many Diphthongs are used ? Which are they ? (1882).

72. How many separate Vowel-sounds are there in English, and how many true Diphthongs? Show in what way defect or redundancy in the Alphabet disguises the true nature and relations of these various sounds. (1873).

73. What various sounds has the letter *a* in English ? How does it come to have so many ? Which of them is the oldest ? (1884).

74. Give examples of the various sounds of *a* in our language; also those of *ough*, and of *ch*. (1887).

75. What various sounds are represented in English by the letter *u* ? (1885).

76. What Vowel-sounds were the letters *a, e, i, o, u*, originally intended to represent? (1882).

77. In what various ways are the letter *g* and the combination *gh* pronounced in English ? How do there come to be various ways ? (1886).

78. Which are the oldest Vowels ? (1886).

79. Select from the following words those in which a true Diphthong, or coalition of two Vowel-sounds, occurs; and give your reason for rejecting the rest: — Belief; Boat; Neuter; Bread; Bounty; Co-operate; Tough; Boot; Boil; Russia. (1869).

80. Classify the Consonants according to their sounds. (1872, 1886).

81. Arrange the Consonants in Classes; and show in what way any of the sounds are related to any of the others. Comment especially on the sounds represented by the letters *h, c, x,* and *j.* (1871).

82. Give a list of the mutes in the English Alphabet, dividing them into Gutturals, Dentals, and Labials, and explain the meaning of those terms. (1858, 1880).

83. Give some account of the letter *c* and its uses. (1885).

84. What is meant by saying that consonants "fall under the category of noises"? (1884).

85. What is meant by *Runes?* Tell whatever you know concerning any runic letters admitted into the English Alphabet. (1881).

86. What would be the ideal of a perfect Alphabet? How far, and in what respects, does the English Alphabet fulfil, or fall short of, that ideal? (1875).

87. How many Letters are there in the English Alphabet? How many Sounds are said to be used in forming English words? What letters are redundant? In the classification of letters what is meant by the terms Vowel, Labial, Guttural, Dental, Flat and Sharp Mutes, Aspirates and Liquids? Make a Table or Tables, arranging the letters under these several heads. (1874).

88. What examples can you give of deficiency, of

unnecessary letters, or of inconsistencies, in the
English Alphabet? Can you account on any principle for the facts?—

(1) That the *s* in "roads" and "robes" is
sounded like *z*;

(2) That the *d* in "hoped" and "missed" is
sounded like *t*;

(3) That the *p* in "Campbell" and "Cupboard"
is scarcely pronounced at all.   (1864).

89. Give some examples of defect and of excess in
the English Alphabet. Comment on any peculiarities in the spelling, or on any incongruity between the spelling and the sound, in the following words:—Thro*ugh*; Miss*ed*; Cu*p*board; D*u*ty;
Bea*u*ty; Mi*ss*ion; Vi*s*ion; *Ch*urch; *Ch*ronology;
Coul*d*; Leed*s*; *Nei*ther.   (1870).

90. Classify the consonants of the English Alphabet, and show whether, regarded as a system of
signs to represent articulate sounds, they are de-
ficient or redundant.   (1861).

91. Classify the sounds used in speaking English,
pointing out those which, in our Alphabet, have the
same letter for their sign.   (1884).

92. For how many sounds are there signs given
by the English Alphabet? How many signs might
be taken to represent all the elementary sounds used
in forming English words? Give a full list of these
sounds classified.   (1880).

93. How many sounds might possibly be represented by the English Alphabet?   (1879).

94. What number of sounds is there in English
to be represented by our Alphabet? Mention any
expedients to which we are driven in order to express them; and show how the difficulties of spelling
are increased thereby.   (1863).

95. State the principal defects in English ortho-

graphy. To what are they due? and how are they remedied? (1868).

96. Illustrate by examples some of the anomalies of English spelling; and state how they arise. (1866).

97. Point out some of the inconsistencies of English Spelling, and of English Pronunciation. How have such inconsistencies arisen? (1887).

98. Give half-a-dozen instances of words of which the present spelling obscures the etymology. How did such spelling come into fashion? (1886).

99. Can you explain the italicised letters in the following words?—Chil*d*ren, woul*d*, coul*d*, again*st*, gen*d*er, victuals, frontispiece, crayfi*sh*, mice. (1836).

100. Discuss the pronunciation of *chivalry, project, humble, Deuteronomy, dynamiter, either.* How do there come to be such different pronunciations of the vowel *a* as are heard in such words as *master?* (1886).

101. Give examples in English Spelling

   (1) Of single letters representing double sounds;

   (2) Of two or more letters representing an indivisible sound;

   (3) Of different letters representing the same sound;

   (4) Of a given letter standing for two or more different sounds;

   (5) Of redundant and of silent letters. (1863).

102. What instances have we in English spelling (1) of true diphthongs spelt with two letters; (2) of single vowel-sounds spelt with two letters; and (3) of true diphthongs represented by single letters? (1860).

103. Mention some articulate sounds which are

incapable of being combined in pronunciation. Give the reason, and show how it explains the formation of plurals and of past tenses in English. (1872).

104. To what letter changes are languages liable? Give examples from the English language (1) of the softening of the guttural, (2) of the substitution of *d* for *th*, (3) of the loss of letters, (4) of the insertion of the letters *b*, *d*. (1878).

105. What consonantal changes have been observed to prevail between cognate words in English and any other allied language? (1879).

106. State Grimm's Law, and give some illustrations of it. (1872).

107. What is meant by Grimm's Law, and to which group does it apply? How would you class the letter *h*? (1887).

108. Tell the history of Grimm's Law. (1880).

109. Give, with a few words of comment, ten illustrations of Grimm's Law. (1884).

110. Our "three" is in Latin "tres," in German "drei." Give some account of the law deduced from such variation in the form of words within the family of languages to which English belongs. (1874).

111. Latin *duo* is English *two* and German *zwei*. Tell what you know of the law which is said to explain changes such as these. (1882).

112. English "*three*" is Latin "*tres*," in German "*drei*." State and explain by examples the law to which a change of this kind is attributed. (1879).

113. What law is illustrated by change of consonant in the words *thou*, *tu*, and (German) *du*? (1871).

114. What laws are said to account (1) for the change of *t* in *pater* to *th* in *father*, (2) for the change of *u* in *thumb* to *i* in *thimble*? (1874).

III. ETYMOLOGY AND INFLECTION.

(MORRIS, Chap. 6).

115. What is Grammar, and why is it so named? (1871).

116. Define the words:—*Grammar, Etymology, Syntax, Gender, Number, Case, Mood,* and *Tense.* (1888).

117. Tell what you know concerning any point of Grammar which seems to you of fundamental importance, choosing that upon which you are most able to give accurate information. (1872).

118. "All our Grammar is thoroughly English, and is not borrowed" (Morris). What does this mean? Arrange the parts of speech; and group together certain classes of terms according to the language from which they are borrowed. (1876).

119. "Ancient languages were more full of declensions, cases, conjugations, and the like; the modern, commonly destitute of them, do loosely deliver themselves in many expressions by prepositions and auxiliary verbs."—*Advancement of Learning.*

Explain this statement, and illustrate it, if you can, by examples. Is the assertion true in relation to the older as compared with the modern forms of *our own language?* (1861).

120. Distinguish between a Syllable and a Word. What is meant by the Parts of Speech? Name them; and show what purpose each serves in the expression of thought. (1875).

121. What exactly is meant by the Phrase "Parts of Speech"? (1883).

122. Name the Parts of Speech. Which of them undergo Inflection? Which are considered the oldest, and which retain most traces of older forms? (1877).

123. Name and define each of the Parts of Speech. (1870, 1879, 1883).

124. Define each of the Parts of Speech, and give the reasons for and against including the article among them. (1872, 1880).

125. Make a list of the Parts of Speech in English in the order of their relative importance, and give reasons for your arrangement. (1861).

126. How many Parts of Speech are there in English? Construct sentences to show how the same word may belong to a different part of speech, according to its use and collocation. (1875).

127. Classify the Parts of Speech; and reduce them to the smallest number of classes consistent with accuracy and completeness. (1866).

128. Classify our Words. Show that to some extent the form of a word indicates its class. Why only "to some extent"? To what class or classes belong *that, ink, after, stand, parallel, good*? (1886).

129. Define a Noun, a Pronoun, an Adjective, and a Verb. What is an Article? Why would you or would you not class it as a distinct Part of Speech? (1874).

130. Explain the origin and exact use of the Articles in English. Discuss the value and necessity of Articles as parts of speech. (1371).

131. Show that the division of words into Parts of Speech is logical and exhaustive. Is there ever any difficulty in deciding what part of speech a word is? If so, why? What are the words itali-

cised in *" Others saw him as* he returned sooner *than* either I or *my* friends " ? (1878).

132. Words have been divided into Notional and Relational. Explain this classification ; and show how it may be made to correspond with the ordinary division of parts of speech. (1872).

133. What are inflections ? How have so many old inflections been lost in English ? and how is their function now supplied in nouns and in verbs respectively ? (1878).

134. How does modern English supply the place of inflections ? State what you know of the order in which they gradually disappeared from the language. Do any traces remain of older forms? (1875).

135. Show what classes of words admit of the most varied inflection, and what classes of words are incapable of it. Comment also on the inflection of the following words :—

Geese ; Pence ; Vixen ; What ; Brethren ; Eldest ; Whom ; Could ; Did ; Themselves ; Stricken ; Worse ; Kept ; Ought. (1864).

136. What traces does the English language retain of the declension of nouns and adjectives ? (1867).

137. What remains of case inflection are to be found in current English ? (1885).

138. Trace any remains of inflection which are to be found in English nouns and pronouns, as in current use. (1888).

139. Make a list of early inflections in nouns or pronouns, which have not survived in modern English ; and give examples. (1873).

140. Mention some words in which the *s* of the stem has been mistaken for the plural flexion. (1887).

141. Give examples of English words in which differences of *(a)* gender, *(b)* number, *(c)* person, *(d)* case, *(e)* mood, *(f)* tense, are marked in the *form* of the word. How is the place of Inflection supplied in English? Give examples. (1866).

IV. The Noun.

(Morris, Chap. 7).

142. Classify the Nouns. (1880).

143. What principles would you adopt in classifying Nouns in English? Explain fully the basis of the classification which you adopt. (1889).

144. Give a Classification of English Nouns. Reduce the Parts of Speech to the smallest possible number. (1869).

145. Explain the meaning of Collective Nouns, Abstract Nouns and Concrete Nouns, and give examples of each. (1858).

146. Give instances of Common Nouns becoming Proper, and of Proper becoming Common. (1881, 1887).

147. What exactly is meant in Grammar by the term *gender*? Are there now any traces of *gender* in English? (1884).

148. Make a list of different ways of expressing Gender in English nouns, adding a few notes on the history of each. (1884).

149. Describe and account for our ways of marking Gender in Nouns. (1875).

150. Describe and illustrate the different ways of marking Gender in English Nouns. (1874).

151. How are distinctions of Gender marked in English? What remains are preserved of obsolete terminations to indicate the feminine? (1875).

152. How is Gender distinguished in modern English? What causes brought about the gradual

disuse of *grammatical* gender after the Norman Conquest? (1878).

153. What was the ancient form of the Feminine Gender? What traces remain of it? How has it been supplanted? Discuss the meaning and origin of the termination—*ster*. (1879).

154. What do you understand by "Gender" in grammar? Show how your definition applies to each of these words:—*Aunt, Sempstress, She, That, Man-servant, Testatrix, Mistress, Heroine, Margravine.* (1873.)

155. On what principle is the gender of English nouns settled? Compare it with the principle of gender in any other language. Which is the more philosophical? (1861).

156. Define the grammatical term *Gender*. What is the original force of the suffix in *Hunter, Maltster?* Account for the gender of *Sun* and *Moon* in modern English. (1881).

157. Describe the several ways of indicating Gender in English nouns, including explanation of the words *woman, lady, vixen, seamstress, mistress, bridegroom, widower, drake.* (1880).

158. Give the history of the form of the plural in English, and account for the variations. How are plurals formed in modern English? Give as full a list as you can of exceptions to the rule. (1877).

159. Give some account of the different plural forms of English Nouns. (1881).

160. Discuss and illustrate all methods of distinguishing Number in English Nouns. How has the use of the suffix *s* as a sign of plurality been accounted for? (1879).

161. Mention the three regular modes of forming the plurals of genuine English words and give examples. (1858).

c 2

162. Show how we came by the plural in *s*. (1379).

163. Show what suffixes have been used to mark the plural in English, and how the number of those in ordinary use has been reduced. (1885).

164. Discuss and illustrate all methods of distinguishing Number in English Nouns. Mention some nouns which have (1) no Singular; (2) no Plural; (3) two Plural forms with different meanings. (1878).

165. Give rules for the plurals of substantives ending in vowels. Of what is the *s* significant in the following words respectively:—Pea*s*; Alm*s*; Riche*s*; Summon*s*? (1877).

166. Mention some nouns (i) with two plural forms, (ii) with no plural form, (iii) with only a plural form, (iv) of plural forms which are treated as singulars, (v) of singular forms which are treated as plurals. (1865, 1886).

167. Give the rules for the formation of plurals in English. State as many exceptions as you can. Discuss especially such forms as *children, brethren,* &c. How did the plural in *s* gain the ascendency? (1876).

168. State fully both the rules and the exceptions for the formation of English plurals. Give six examples of nouns which have two plurals with different meanings. (1876).

169. How are English plurals formed? Give examples of anomalous and of obsolete formations. Give instances of nouns that vary their meaning with their Number. (1868).

170. Mention any English nouns which form their plurals by processes generally obsolete. Which of the following are genuine plurals, and how do you account for the forms which are not such: *Alms, Summons, Banns, Sessions, Costs, Eaves, Weeds, Riches, Dice?* (1881).

171. Write down some nouns that have no special form to express plurality. (1883).

172. It is said that *abstract* nouns have no plural *form*. Explain this statement, and account for forms like " negligences," " benevolences," &c. (1863).

173. Take following forms, and state from them the rules for forming English plurals :—*Men, kine, churches, animalcula, sons-in-law.* (1866).

174. Tell what you know about nouns forming their plurals in *en.* (1879).

175. Discuss the plural form *children.* (1883).

176. What are the following as to number— *children, scissors, riches, alms, means, news, fire-arms, amends, pains, dice, pence?* State which are used as singulars, and which as plurals, or as both. (1859).

177. Give the plural forms of *brother, cargo, valley, strife, seraph, virtuoso, madame, memorandum, fish, penny, vesper, Mr. Thomson, yea.* Comment on the forms which violate the common rules. (1868).

178. Give the plurals of *lady, valley, loaf, strife ;* and of the following Latin and Greek words used in English : *formula, radius, phenomenon, analysis.* (1858).

179. Write down the plural form of *wharf, colloquy, potato, Mary, Knight Templar, canto,* and state and discuss the rule you go by in each case. (1887).

180. Explain, as precisely as you can, the origin of the plural *s,* and of any other plural forms, in English nouns. (1872).

181. Discuss each of these plural forms : *leaves, oxen, kine, men, brethren ;* also the forms, *news, pains, riches, eaves, summons.* (1884).

182. What English nouns make no change in the plural number, and why ? (1888).

183. What does *Case* mean ? Define it so as to suit an inflected, and a non-inflected, Language respectively. By what various ways do we know that a noun is in the Object case in modern English ? (1877).

184. Explain the terms *declension, case,* and illustrate each by an example. (1871).

185. It has been said that in English nouns there is no objective case. Criticise this statement. (1871).

186. Give the origin and meaning of the word *case.* What is the real power of the genitive case ? Explain the following forms :—*Their, Golden,* For Christ *his* sake. (1882).

187. Define Case. State how many Case-endings there are in English Nouns, and how many relics of Case-endings in other parts of speech. Give examples. (1868).

188. Tell the history of each of the forms now used for the Inflection of Nouns. (1871).

189. What is the origin, and what is the meaning in English grammar, of the term *Case*? Of what lost case-endings are the traces still discernible in our language ? (1881).

190. What cases had nouns formerly in English ? Which of them still formally exist ? Of how many of them can the force still be expressed by the simple form of the word without a preposition ? Give full examples. (1879).

191. Mention the Case-endings which still exist in English Nouns and Pronouns. (1858).

192. What is meant by Case in nouns ? Tell the history of the Possessive Case in English, and define the present limits of its use. (1882).

193. How does the Possessive case differ from the Genitive ? (1887).

194. What relations are expressed by the Genitive case ? (1859).

195. What does *Genitive* mean? Why was the Possessive Case so called? Trace the growth of that case in modern English from earlier forms, singular and plural. What letter and letters does the Apostrophe represent, and what is its value in pronunciation, in—*Man's*; *Fish's*; *Cow's*; *Hero's*; *James's*; *Jesus'*; *Men's*; *Mice's*; *Friend's*; *Banditti's*. (1877).

196. What different Genitive forms have we in English? Which is the more ancient; and when is each the more appropriate? What is an Objective genitive? (1867).

197. Show how we came by the Possessive Case in *'s*. (1879).

198. Explain, as precisely as you can, the origin of the genitive in *'s*. (1872).

199. Which is the more ancient form, "father's" or "of a father"? (1859).

200. How is the Possessive Case formed in nouns ending in *-s*? Discuss the form "for goodness' sake." How is the possessive formed in compound nouns, or noun phrases? (1878).

201. Describe and account for the loss of Inflections in English Nouns, with special reference to the inflections that remain. (1880).

202. Define "gender" and "case." In what case, as to *form*, are "once" and "seldom"? Give any similar forms in English. (1859).

203. Describe and account for the present methods of representing Number and Case in our nouns. (1875).

204. What is the meaning of the words *Declension* and *Case* respectively? How is the Possessive Case denoted in English? What does *Genitive* mean? Addison observes:—"The single letter *s* on many occasions does the office of a whole word, and represents the *his* and *her* of our forefathers."

Explain and illustrate the confusion involved in this statement.   (1877).

205. Define Number, Gender, and Case; and state how far your definition applies to English only, or also to any other language.   (1870).

206. Describe and account for the different methods of indicating Case, Gender, and Number in nouns.   (1874).

V. The Adjective and Numerals.

(Morris, Chap. 8).

207. How is a word known to be an Adjective? (1865).

208. Classify English Adjectives according to their terminations. Explain the force of these terminations, and state which of them are susceptible of being varied to indicate Comparison. (1877).

209. Give a definition of an Adjective which shall include *tall, third, nine, some, the.* Classify Adjectives according to their functions, and explain the force and origin of the endings, *-ly, -ish, -ine, -en, -y, -al, -ic, -ous, -less, -some.* (1878).

210. Give examples of Adjectives which have come to be used as nouns. (1865).

211. Give some examples of irregular Adjectives in English, and account for their forms. How far is it incorrect to describe any such forms as irregular? (1873).

212. Have we in English any Adjectives that govern a case? If so, what? Give six Adjectives with irregular comparative forms. (1863).

213. Are English Adjectives ever declinable? (1865).

214. What is the difference in meaning between *monitory* and *monetary, definite* and *definitive, credible,* and *creditable, confident* and *confidant, virtuous* and *virtual, expedient* and *expeditious?* (1886).

215. Mention some cognates of *better, nether, among, noun, rather, toward.* (1886).

216. What arguments might be used for and

against the recognition of the Article as a distinct part of speech? Tell what you know of the history of *an* and *the*. (1880).

217. Tell what you know of the history and present use of *a* and *the*. How would you place them among the parts of speech, and why? (1881).

218. Tell the history of the forms *a, an,* and *the,* and discuss their grammatical use. (1874, 1883).

219. Illustrate our habit of using Nouns both with and without change of form, and also of using Adverbs as Adjectives. (1887).

220. How are Degrees of Comparison formed? Give examples (1) of Adjectives irregularly compared; (2) of Adjectives comparative in form, but not so used. (1877).

221. In what two ways may Adjectives be compared? How do there come to be two ways? By what terms would you denote them? State the general rule as to their use. (1887).

222. How are Degrees of Comparison formed in English? Give six examples of irregular formations. Of what word is *First* the superlative? (1869).

223. How are Degrees of Comparison formed in English? Account for the irregular forms. Of what word is *first* the superlative, and *rather* the comparative? (1875).

224. Show the different forms employed for marking comparison in Adjectives, and explain the origin and exact import of the most usual forms. (1889).

225. State fully what Adjectives can now be compared by terminations, and to what modifications the Positive is liable. Distinguish in meaning and origin between *further* and *farther, later* and *latter, elder* and *older*. (1878).

226. Which are the usual suffixes of comparison in English? Mention any English words now in use in which other comparative suffixes are visible. Explain the forms *Next* ; *Farthest* ; *Foremost*. (1882).

227. Describe and account for the regular and irregular forms of comparison in Adjectives. (1880).

228. Write down those Adjectives which are defective in their comparison. (1888).

229. Discuss Comparative and Superlative forms of Adjectives, and explain the forms *worse, next, first, farthest, furthest*. (1881).

230. Classify Adjectives irregularly compared. Give the Positive and Superlative of *More* ; *Farther* ; *Former* ; *Utter* ; *Hinder* ; *Less* ; *Rather* ; *Further* ; *Latter* ; *Nearer* ; and tell what you know of the history of each. (1879).

231. Give some examples of irregular forms of comparison. (1865, 1872).

232. Discuss any five examples of what is called Irregular Comparison in Adjectives. What Adjectives cannot properly be used in the Comparative or Superlative degree? (1879).

233. Give seven examples of Irregular Comparison in Adjectives, and tell what you know of their history. (1874).

234. Quote and discuss any six examples of Irregular Comparison in Adjectives. (1874).

235. Discuss ten examples of what is called Irregular Comparison in Adjectives. (1882)..

236. Give as many examples as you can of Adjectives irregularly compared. Indicate traces in Modern English of Comparison marked by Vowel-change. What is *-most* when used as a suffix? How do you account for such a form as *furthermore*? (1876).

237. Which English Adjectives cannot be compared? (1888).

238. Examine the forms *lesser, worse, foremost, elder, farther.* (1883).

239. What is the meaning of Adjective-endings in *-er*? Give a list of irregular superlative forms. (1868).

240. Of what word is "first" the superlative? (1865).

241. Give the positive forms of *more, further, worse, rather, less*; and add any explanations you deem important. (1865).

242. Explain the following forms:—*First; Worse; Best; Next; Last; More; Less; Rather.* Distinguish between *Later* and *Latter; Further* and *Farther; Elder* and *Older.* (1868).

243. Distinguish between *farther* and *further, gladder* and *gladlier, nearest* and *next, latest* and *last, peas* and *pease, genii* and *geniuses.* (1887).

244. Explain as fully as you can the superlative forms *inmost, next, best, least, last, first,* and the comparative forms *nearer* and *worse.* (1883).

245. Give some examples of double superlatives. (1872).

246. What are the positive and superlative of *more, nearer, rather, less, former, utter?* Give explanations of these forms and of *uttermost* and *inmost.* (1866).

247. Explain the formation of comparative and superlative in the adjectives *good, bad, much, little, far* and *near.* (1873).

248. Define Cardinal, Ordinal, and Distributive Numerals. What Numerals are not of Saxon origin? Give the derivation of *eleven, twelve* and *both,* respectively. How does *both* differ from *two*? (1866).

249. Define Cardinal, Ordinal, and Distributive

Numerals. Give explanations of each. Give the derivation of *Five, Eleven, Twelve, Both*. (1875).

250. What are Cardinal and Ordinal Numbers? Explain the origin and formation of the words *first, second, third, fourth, eleven, twelve*. (1872).

251. What are Cardinal and Ordinal Numbers? Explain the forms *eleven* and *twelve*, the endings of numbers in *-teen* and *-ty*, and the words *hundred* and *thousand*. Account for the method of forming Ordinals. (1881).

252. What is a Cardinal Number ? Distinguish between the forms *two* and *twain*. Discuss the origin of the words *ten, eleven, twelve, hundred, thousand, dozen, score*. (1884).

253. Account for the separate forms *two* and *twain*, and the words *ten, eleven, twelve, hundred, thousand, first, second, dozen, score, fortnight*. (1880).

VI. The Pronoun.

(Morris, Chap. 9).

254. What exactly is meant by a " Pronoun "? (1885).

255. Discuss the ordinary definition of a Pronoun. What other definition has been suggested ? (1887).

256. Classify the Pronouns, and tell something of the history of their inflections.   (1868, 1872, 1874, 1875, 1876, 1877, 1879, 1880, 1884).

257. Make a list of English Pronouns, classifying them according to the system which you prefer. Point out any examples of true inflection which your list contains.   (1864).

258. How are Pronouns and Adjectives distinguished ?   (1866).

259. Account for the greater permanence of case-endings in Pronouns than in Adjectives.   Describe generally the pronominal case-endings and tell something of their history.   (1884).

260. Cite some examples of the remains of obsolete inflection in English Pronouns.   (1871).

261. What was the original number and case of *you*?   Discuss the history of this word fully. (1878).

262. Tell what you know of the past and present use of the Second Personal Pronoun in its Nominative and Accusative Cases, singular and plural. (1882).

263. Trace as fully as you can the history of the inflections of *thou*, and of *he, she, it*, in singular and plural.   (1880).

264. Tell what you know of the introduction of the genitive form *its*. (1873).

265. When did *its* first come into use? How had its place been previously supplied? (1876).

266. What significance lies in the italicised letters of the following?—Hi*m* ; *s*he ; i*t* ; our*s*. (1876).

267. Tell what you know of the Inflections of the Third Personal Pronoun in singular and plural. (1882).

268. "And that same eye . . . . did lose *his* lustre." (*Julius Cæsar*) :—"Go to *it* Grandam, child " (*King John*) :— " Heaven grant us *its* peace " (*Measure for Measure*). Explain these three forms of the neuter genitive of the Third Personal Pronoun. (1872).

269. Define Reflexive Pronouns. (1882).

270. Explain the construction of *Self*. What part of speech is it? Trace its history. (1879).

271. Trace the history, explain the forms, and determine the meanings, of *self* in its various collocations, singular and plural. (1877).

272. Discuss the meaning of the syllable *self*. Give some reasons for determining whether it should be regarded as a noun or as an adjective. (1872).

273. Explain fully the constructions and inflections of the word " self." (1865).

274. Discuss fully the nature and origin of the forms *Myself* ; *Itself* ; *Himself* ; *Ourselves*. (1867, 1868).

275. State and explain the anomalies and. difficulties observable in various forms of pronouns compounded with various forms of the word -*self*. (1869).

276. Give a complete list of English Possessive Pronouns, stating in regard to each its origin and the period when it first came to be used. (1889).

277. What do you know concerning the origin and history of English Possessive Pronouns? Account for the form *Ours*. (1881).

278. Discuss the significance of the italicised portions of Ou*rs*, Mi*ne*. (1877).

279. Explain the form *Yours* truly. (1882).

280. Distinguish between the forms *my* and *mine*. Which is the older form? What similar pairs are there? (1868, 1887).

281. Explain fully the meanings and uses of *the* in modern English. What was the word originally? How was it inflected? and what traces of its inflection are still found in the language? (1877).

282. What is *the*? Explain and illustrate *all* its uses. What words were originally inflections or derivatives of *the*? State their present use and trace their history. (1878).

283. What is the precise use and force of the English Articles, and how are they derived? (1870).

284. State the arguments in favour of regarding the English Article as a distinct Part of Speech, and also any arguments on the other side. (1888).

285. What Indefinite Article do you use before *history, historical, European, usual, humble, ever?* Give your reasons for your answers. (1887).

286. Can you mention any instances of the transference of the *n* of the indefinite article to the beginning of the following noun? (1887).

287. What exactly is meant by a "Relative Pronoun?" (1885).

288. Make a table of English Relatives, and mention any words derived from them. (1864).

289. Point out and explain different uses of the word *that*. Explain the origin and present use of the words *what, which, whether*. (1881).

290. Tell what you can of the history, and discuss

the various grammatical uses, of the words *that, which, what.* (1882, 1883).

291. What pronouns were originally used where *Relatives* are now employed in our language? (1882).

292. Give rules for the use of *who, that,* and *which,* respectively. What kind of pronouns were these words originally? Give some account of the process by which, and the times at which, they severally came to be used as Relatives. (1877).

293. Distinguish between *which* and *that* as Relatives. (1873).

294. When is the relative *that* used in preference to *who* or *which*? (1867, 1868, 1875).

295. Mention any differences in usage between *who* and *that.* (1885).

296. Is there any difference in usage between *each* and *every*? (1887).

297. Why should you not say "Neither of the ten suited me"? (1887).

298. What alternative form of expression is there to "That is mine and nobody else's"? Which do you think is to be preferred? (1887).

299. Discuss, with reference to their history, the words *ye* and *you, her, its, this, that, which.* (1880).

300. Take the Personal, Possessive, Interrogative, and Relative Pronouns, and show, with examples, which of them can be used *substantively,* which *adjectively,* and which in *both* constructions. (1878).

301. What is an Indefinite Pronoun? Write a list of the chief Indefinite Pronouns, and give the derivation of each of them. (1884).

302. Give a list of Indefinite Pronouns; and tell the derivation of each of these words:—*aught, each, every, either, other.* (1874).

303. Discuss the significance of the italicised letters in ei*ther.* (1877).

D

304. What error has crept into the phrases "ever so many," "to do no more than one can help," "these sort of things"? Suggest some explanation of *mine* in such phrases as "a friend of *mine*." (1886).

VII. The Verb.

(Morris, Chap. 10).

305. Repeat and criticise the current definition of a verb. Which seems to you the least unsatisfactory, and why? (1881, 1887).

306. Classify the Verbs. (1880).

307. Into how many classes may verbs be divided? (1876).

308. Give as many different classifications as you know of English Verbs. Which do you prefer, and why? (1878).

309. Explain and illustrate what is meant by a Transitive verb, an Impersonal verb, a Passive and a Deponent verb. Illustrate the government of each. (1866).

310. What are Transitive Verbs? Are intransitive verbs or passive verbs ever connected in English with an accusative case? Give illustrations. (1863).

311. Show how frequently in English Transitive Verbs are used Intransitively, and *vice versa.* (1887).

312. Write eight sentences giving four examples of the use of the same verb transitively and intransitively. Rewrite the four sentences containing transitive verbs with change of voice from Active to Passive. (1884).

313. Explain the terms Conjugation, Mood, Tense, Participle, Gerund; and illustrate each by an example. (1871).

314. Describe fully, with examples, English Verbs of Incomplete Predication. (1888).

315. Mention some Causative verbs. (1887).

316. Explain the terms: Voice, Mood, Infinitive. (1868, 1876, 1887).

317. Define *Infinitive, Gerund, Present Participle,* and *Past Participle;* giving examples of each. (1888).

318. Distinguish between the Indicative and Subjunctive Moods. (1875).

319. How is the Subjunctive Mood indicated in English? (1868).

320. Write some notes upon the present use of the Subjunctive Mood in English. (1884).

321. Enumerate the elements of flexion in the Verb. What is the use of the Subjunctive Mood? Account for the way in which it is distinguished in English. (1882).

322. What is a Gerund? (1875).

323. Give some account of the history of English Verbal Nouns and Adjectives. (1875).

324. Define the term Tense. (1868, 1876).

325. How many Moods and Tenses are there? (1876).

326. Explain what is meant by Tense and Mood of Verbs. Add a few notes upon past and present forms of the Future Tense and of the Subjunctive Mood in English Verbs, and on the present use of the Subjunctive. (1880).

327. Define Mood and Tense, and show the distinction between the ideas they express and those expressed by the Adverbs of manner and time. (1878).

328. Of how many modifications in respect to time is a verb susceptible? Show how far these modifications are recognised in English accidence; and compare our language in regard to the completeness of its tenses with any other language which you know. (1873).

329. What is Tense? Is English comparatively

rich or poor in its distinction of tenses ? Make a
scheme showing all the varieties of tense of the
verbs *am* and *sing*. (1878).

330. Give the fullest subdivision of an English
Verb into Tenses that you may have met with in
any grammar. Which of those Tenses are distinguished by inflections? (1884).

331. What *tense-forms* have we in English for
calling attention to the continuousness of an act ?
What are indefinite forms? and what emphatic
forms ? (1862).

332. What are Indefinite forms of a Tense ?
What continuous ? (1867).

333. What are the Indefinite, the Continuous or
Imperfect, and the Perfect or complete forms of the
Tenses of English Verbs ? (1870).

334. What different forms of the Present Tense
have we in English? and how do they differ in
meaning ? Explain the form, "Duncan *comes* to-
night." (1866).

335. Describe different ways of forming the Past
Tense in English Verbs, and tell something of their
history. (1874).

336. What traces are there in English of a Perfect formed by reduplication ? Can you show by
what process reduplication has disappeared? (1885).

337. What traces of reduplication would you
adduce in the tense formations of English Verbs?
(1889).

338. Show how a classification of verbs may be
founded upon differences in the form of the Past
Tense? (1882).

339. Discuss the following Past Tenses of
Verbs:—*loved, taught, ate, sang*. Tell what you
know of the forms *ought* and *must*. (1879).

340. Give the past tenses of the verbs *fall, seethe,
eat, fell, seek, set, lie*. (1860).

341. How is the Future Indefinite Tense expressed in English? Illustrate your answer by an examination of the original meaning of the auxiliaries employed for the purpose. Explain the term—the *imperfect continuous* tense. Analyse the forms *could, had, might.* (1882).

342. It has been said that in English Verbs there is no Future Tense. Criticise this statement. (1871).

343. Conjugate the Future Tense of any Verb. (1867).

344. Distinguish between *shall* and *will* as signs of a Future Tense. (1884).

345. Give a rule for the use of *shall* and *will* in Future forms. (1867).

346. Mention some verbs that, being originally preterites, have come to be used as presents. Can you account for such a usage? (1883).

347. How are Number and Person indicated in English Verbs? (1875).

348. State the rules for forming the Third Person Singular in English Verbs. (1868).

349. What traces remain in modern English of the Suffixes added to English Verbs in earlier stages of the language? (1877).

350. What is the origin of the *d* in the Preterite of *love*? What of the *d* in its Past Participle? Explain the forms *had, made, left, built, clad, methinks.* (1886).

351. We write *he thinks*; why do we not write *he musts*? Illustrate your answer by reference to some other verbs. (1881).

352. Explain fully how Number and Person are indicated in English verbs. (1867).

353. Describe our two Conjugations. Which is the living one? Does any verb belong to both? What traces are there of Reduplication? (1886).

354. Explain the terms "strong" and "weak" as applied to verbs; also the term *conjugation*. To which conjugation do you assign *teach, fight, work, do, fly, flow, flee, till, tell, toll*? (1883).

355. What is meant by the terms "strong" and "weak" applied to the Conjugation of Verbs? Explain the difference between the two forms of conjugation by telling what you know about their history. (1880).

356. Distinguish between *Strong* and *Weak* Verbs, and show the peculiarity of tense-formation in regard to each class. (1889).

357. Distinguish between the Strong and the Weak Conjugations. By what other names are they known? Which is the older? Which is the living one? (1887).

358. What are the characteristic marks of the Strong Conjugation? (1887).

359. Distinguish between Weak and Strong Verbs. Is this an exhaustive classification? If not, show what other classes of verbs exist, and give some examples of each. (1870).

360. What are *Strong* Verbs? and to what element of our Language do they belong? Mention any *Weak* verbs that once belonged to this class. (1861).

361. Distinguish between Strong and Weak Conjugations of Verbs; and explain the origin of such past tenses as *ate, held, woke, ran, wrote,* and *flew*. (1875).

362. What are Weak Verbs? Classify *Bring; Sing; Take; Seek; Teach; Set; Bleed; Eat,* as Weak or Strong verbs. Give reasons in each case, and call attention to peculiarities. (1879).

363. To which conjugation do the following verbs severally belong:—*see, saw, say, sow, sew, sue, set, sit, seethe, sell*? Write down the Past Tense and the

Past Participle of each one, noticing any irregularities. (1885).

364. To which Conjugation do these verbs belong?—*fight, think, bare, bear, catch, teach, reach, beseech, hang, fly.* (1887).

365. To which Conjugation belong the verbs—*have, go, read, fall, think, fight, hang, send, wash, feel?* (1886).

366. What is meant by Weak and Strong Verbs, respectively? Give examples. Give the first person of the Perfect, and the Past Participle, of the following:—*Cleave* (in both senses); *smite; tear; thrive; spin; swing; lay; load.* (1876).

367. What are the marks of a "strong" Verb? About how many of such verbs have we still in use? To which conjugation belong *shall, buy, fight, reach, teach?* Can you explain the difference of vowel in the Preterite of *tell?* (1884).

368. Make a list of all the flexions the English verb has now left it. How is it there are so few, and how do we manage to get on with them? (1886).

369. Distinguish between the forms of inflection in Weak and Strong Verbs, and give what reason you can for the difference. Of each of the inflected forms of a Weak Verb tell what you know of its history, and of its use in the expression of thought. (1880).

370. How do you explain the formation of the suffixes which mark the tense in Weak Verbs? (1885).

371. What is the origin and significance of the suffix of the Past Tense of Weak Verbs? (1876, 1888).

372. Make a list of some half-dozen Weak Verbs that have vowel change in the Past Tense; also of half-a-dozen that have no change there, also of half-

a-dozen that do change, but not in the way of addition. (1887).

373. What was the early use of the Infinitive? When was it first distinguished by the prefix "to "? (1885).

374. Why is the "Infinitive" Mood so called? Show in how many ways the Infinitive may be used, and compare the modern English Infinitive either with that of Old English, or with that of any other language you know. (1871).

375. What is meant by the Infinitive Mood? Tell what you know of the past and present use of *to* in the Infinitive. (1873, 1879, 1881).

376. Explain as fully as you can the Infinitive form in the phrase, "This House to Let." (1879).

377. Account for the use of *to* in the Infinitive Present, and for its occasional omission in an Infinitive after a verb; as, "*I dare say.*" (1880).

378. Discuss the difference of usage in such phrases as "I dare say," and "I ought to say." (1873).

379. What part of speech is the Infinitive? What is meant by Dative Infinitive and the Simple Infinitive? Show the origin of the suffixes in "the hang*ing* crane," and "the hang*ing* of the crane." (1882).

380. Discuss the origin and the grammatical use of the Gerundial Infinitive. (1882).

381. How are Infinitives in -*ing* distinguished from Participles? (1868).

382. How are Participles in -*ing* distinguished from Infinitives in -*ing*? What is meant by a Gerundial Infinitive? and what are the peculiarities of its government? (1866).

383. How do you distinguish Participles in -*ing* from common Infinitives in -*ing* and from Gerundial Infinitives? (1868).

384. Explain the differences of the verbal form which ends in -*ing*, and show in what cases it is properly a Participle. (1888).

385. State what you know of the origin, forms, and uses of English Gerunds. (1876).

386. What is meant by the Infinitive Mood of a Verb? Distinguish between Gerund and Participle. (1872).

387. What is a Participle? (1875).

388. What are Participles? From what words are they derived? by what terminations are they known? and to what uses are they applied in the formation of sentences? (1861).

389. Give four verbs that have but one form for the Present Tense, the Past Tense, and the Complete Participle. Give four that have two forms, and six that have three. (1861).

390. Give the Preterites and Past Participles of the following verbs : *forsake, hang, feed, freeze, tread, slide, spin, spit, bid, abide, find, throw, see.* (1858).

391. Give the Perfect Tense and Past Participle of the following verbs :—*Shear, lie, lade, be, chide, freight, cleave, thrive, swing, slide, spring, swim.* (1869).

392. Give the Past Tense and Past Participle of the following :—*fall, shoe, sing, knot, ride, know, jump, go, tear, steal, sit, slit.* (1860).

393. Give the Past Tense and the Complete Participle of the following words :—*Eat, sit, slit, shut, bleed, lie, lay, sew, strew.* (1865).

394. Give the Past and Perfect Tenses of *sit; sew; shrink; thrive; lend; run; lead; lie; set; lay; swing; seethe;* and give the Past Tense of the following :—"I *dare* do all that may become a man;" and "I *ought to know.*" (1867).

395. Give the Perfect Tense and Past Participle of *climb, cleave, forego, lay, lie, smite, swim, speed, heave, slink, cling, shake, tear, flee.* (1875).

396. Give the Past Tense and the Complete Participle of *lie down, lay, freight, hide, shear, sew, saw, see, sit, set, put, bid.* (1868).

397. Give the Past Tense and the Complete Participle of *set, sit, see, sweat, swing, eat, lie, lay, do.* (1862).

398. What is an Irregular Verb? Show how far it is possible to classify, or to reduce to rule, many so-called irregular verbs. Is there any form of irregularity which might more properly be explained as Defectiveness? Give examples. (1869).

399. Make a classified list of the Irregular Verbs. (1860).

400. Give three specimens of each of the classes into which English Irregular Verbs are divided. (1870).

401. Give some account of the Verbs called Irregular, and explain the inflections of any two of them. (1874).

402. Give some examples of "irregular" Verbs and Adjectives; and explain how the irregularity may be accounted for. Is there any connection between "Defectiveness" and "Irregularity" in Grammar? (1864).

403. Give some examples of Irregular Verbs in English, and account for their forms. How far is it incorrect to describe any such forms as Irregular? (1873).

404. What is the difference between Irregular and Defective Verbs? Give examples to explain your meaning. Explain the formation of *could* and *wert.* (1866).

405. What Verbs have been called Auxiliary? What is meant by a Verb Substantive? Tell the history of the inflections of the verb "to be." (1874).

406. Give a list of the Auxiliary Verbs in the

English language, and show (1) the original meaning of each as an independent verb; (2) its signification and use as an auxiliary. Point out the difference in the ordinary use of the words *shall* and *will* as auxiliaries, and explain the reason of that difference. (1860).

407. Which are the English Auxiliary Verbs properly so called? Explain the forms of the Preterites of the verbs, *Have, Make, Can.* (1881).

408. Give some account of the past history and present use of the verbs *shall* and *will.* (1873).

409. Conjugate the verbs " shall " and " will." State the rules for their use. Give example of the correct and of the incorrect use of them. (1865).

410. State the correct modérn usage of *shall* and *will*; and show by reference to the etymology of these words, how that usage is to be accounted for. (1888).

411. Give some account of the different forms of the verb *to be.* (1879).

412. Comment on the verb " To be "; and tell what you know of the history of its inflections. (1875).

413. To what uses do we put the verb "to be" in the English language? (1864).

414. What are the different uses of the verb *To be*? From how many verbs are the parts of this verb formed? (1879).

415. What part is taken by the Verb *Have* in conjugating English Verbs? Explain the process by which *Have* came to be so used, and discuss the following:—I *have* a letter; I *have* written a letter; I *have* come to post it; the post *is* gone. (1879).

416. How do you connect the primary meaning with the auxiliary use of *have*? (1876).

417. Why is the " Verb Substantive" so called? From what three roots are its various parts respec-

tively derived? Write down its Subjunctive Mood. (1877).

418. What do you know of the verbs *quoth, wot, thinks* in methinks? (1887).

419. What three origins has our "substantive verb?" Explain *worth* in "woe *worth* the day." Mention some usages in which "am" as an auxiliary has been ousted by "have." (1885).

420. What were the original meanings, respectively, of *have; be; can; shall; may; must; will;* when used as principal verbs? and how has the meaning been modified in each case by their use as Auxiliaries? (1869).

421. Explain the formation of the following Auxiliary Verbs:—*Shall, must, durst, could, should, ought.* (1885).

422. Account for the formation of the following Auxiliary Verbs:—*May, can, will, could, ought, might, hast, must.* (1888).

423. When is *dare* inflected in the 3rd sing. Pres. Ind.? Can you cast any light on the forms *durst, wist, wrought, sold, sought, ago?* (1886).

424. Why may we not say, "He cans do it?" (1886).

425. Take the words *can, be, must, shall, have, may* and *will;* and say (1) what is the original meaning of each, and (2) how much, if any, of that meaning is still retained in its use as an Auxiliary Verb. (1871).

426. Discuss the inflections of the verbs *may, can, shall, have, will, do.* (1880).

427. Discuss the verbs *shall, will, can* and *may,* with reference to their inflections and to their past and present use as parts of sentences. (1880).

428. Explain peculiarities in conjugation of the verbs *be, go, ought, must.* (1873).

429. What are the various meanings of the verb

owe? In what different ways is it conjugated? (1876).

430. Discuss the various uses, forms, meanings, and constructions of the verbs *do, own* and *think*, respectively. Give examples. (1876).

431. Give examples of verbs that are used both as " complete " and "incomplete predicates"; and explain these terms. (1883).

432. What is the force of *run* in such a phrase as "to run wild," of *wear* in "the day wears," of *give* in "the shoe gives," of *obtain* in "this doctrine obtained," of *take* in "take offence"? Mention any noticeable uses of *to taste, ring, sit, stand, go.* (1883).

433. Explain, with reference to their origin, the use of the words *own* and *owe*, in "I *own* a pound," "I *owe* a pound," and "I *own* I *owe* a pound." Explain the verbs in the question "How *do* you *do*?" (1884).

434. Which form would you prefer to use: He *dare* not, or He *dares* not? What is to be said on behalf of each form? Explain the forms *willy nilly, won't, to wit.* (1884).

VIII. ADVERBS, PREPOSITIONS AND CONJUNCTIONS.

(MORRIS, Chaps. 11-13).

435. Discuss fully the meaning and origin of the Inseparable Particles. (1877).

436. What is an Adverb? Give examples of adverbs derived from numerals, from nouns, and from other adverbs. In what other ways are adverbs formed? (1874).

437. Classify English Adverbs. (1875, 1881).

438. Classify Adverbs (a) as to the ideas they express, (b) as to their origin. (1879).

439. Classify Adverbs with reference to their signification. (1875).

440. Classify English Adverbs, (1) according to their *origin*, (2) according to their *meaning*. How many Parts of Speech can Adverbs qualify? Parse *By little and little: at unawares.* (1878).

441. Classify adverbs as to their *form*, and as to their *meaning*. (1861).

442. Write down in separate columns Adverbs (1) of place, (2) time, (3) manner, and (4) degree. (1876).

443. Show how Adverbs may be classified according to their meaning. Why are *Yes* and *No* placed among Adverbs? (1884).

444. Make two classifications of Adverbs; one logical, according to their meaning; the other etymological, according to their form and origin. (1880).

445. Tell what you can of the origin and grammatical use of the words *yea, yes, aye, nay, no.* (1881).

446. Distinguish between Adjectives and Adverbs, exemplifying your answer by illustrative sentences. (1860, 1861).

447. Give examples of a Prepositional and a Pronominal Adverb, and of an Adverb formed by the genitive singular of a substantive. (1882).

448. Point out the different ways in which Adverbs have been formed from Nouns, from Pronouns, and from Adjectives. (1882).

449. Tabulate the Adverbs connected with the stems *he*, *the*, *who*, and explain their formation and meaning. (1877).

450. What Adverbs take degrees of comparison? (1868).

451. Explain the true import and construction of *than*, in comparative sentences. (1878).

452. Discuss fully the various uses of *as* and *than*. (1876).

453. What is "than" after a comparative? and by what case is it followed? Criticise the following:—"Than whom none higher sat" (*Milton*). (1862).

454. Explain the construction of *than* in comparative sentences, and illustrate your meaning fully by examples. (1866).

455. What are *no* and *the* before a comparative? (1875).

456. What are Adverbial Clauses? Give examples. (1861).

457. What is an Adverbial Clause? and what parts of speech can it qualify? (1870).

458. Explain the forms *To-morrow*; I and the lad will go *yonder*; *The* more *the* merrier. (1882).

459. What are Prepositions? Make some classification of them founded on the different relations they express. (1874, 1886).

460. Classify English Prepositions (1) according

to their Meaning, and (2) according to their Forms. (1875, 1876).

461. Classify Prepositions as simple and compound. Analyse the compound ones. Show, with illustrations, what Prepositions can be used adverbially. (1877).

462. Take six of our common English Prepositions, and after showing of each, as nearly as you can, its original meaning, show in what way it has been taken to represent different relations of place, time, and causality. (1883).

463. What are "Verbal Prepositions"? Give six examples, and show how they came to be used prepositionally. (1878, 1879).

464. Give an example of a Preposition formed by the past participle of a verb. (1882).

465. Write some short sentences to show the various meanings of the Prepositions *at, with, of, from, against.* Explain "He did his duty *by* him," "*under* these circumstances," "ten *to* one it is not so," "add ten *to* one," "keep up *for* my sake." (1885).

466. Append the appropriate Prepositions to the following :—*Independent, difference, agree, averse, dissent, correspond, conformable.* (1862).

467. Distinguish the meaning of the following combinations :—Conversant *with* and *in* ; confide *in* and *to* ; agree *to* and *with* ; differ *from*, differ *with*, difference *between*. (1862).

468. Classify Conjunctions with reference to their signification. (1875).

469. Classify the Conjunctions as to the kind of sentences which they connect. How do you account for the use of "*that*" in—"He says *that* he is ready"? (1877).

470. Classify the Conjunctions, and point out which of them are used in forming co-ordinate sentences. (1881).

E

471. Classify Conjunctions with reference to (*a*) their use; (*b*) their origin. (1887).

472. How are Conjunctions most conveniently classified? Do they connect sentences only, or words also? Justify your answer. (1867).

473. Distinguish between Co-ordinating and Subordinating Conjunctions. Which are the various uses of the word *But* in English? (1881).

474. What are Correlative Conjunctions? Give the correlatives of *either, though, both,* and of *such* and *so* with different senses. (1862).

475. How do Adverbs differ from Conjunctions? (1876).

476. Point out the difference between an Adverb and a Conjunction; and give examples of words used both as adverbs and conjunctions. (1868).

477. Distinguish between Conjunctions and Prepositions, exemplifying your answer by illustrative sentences. (1860, 1861).

478. How do you distinguish Prepositions, Conjunctions and Adverbs? (1866, 1867, 1870, 1886).

479. Give examples of *But* as an adverb, a preposition, a relative, and a conjunction. (1868).

480. Write two sentences showing the same word used in one as a Preposition, in the other as a Conjunction; also two sentences showing the same word used as a Preposition and as an Adverb. (1879).

481. Mention some Prepositions that have become Conjunctions. (1886).

482. Why are Interjections not to be reckoned as Parts of Speech? (1882).

IX. Syntax.

483. Define the province, in Grammar, of Ortho- ?
graphy, Etymology, and Syntax. (1861).

484. What is the proper province of Syntax in
Grammar? Quote and illustrate those rules both of
Concord and Government which appear to you to be
fundamental and most important. (1863).

485. Define Syntax, and quote those Syntactical
rules which you consider *fundamental* in English
Grammar. Explain also to what extent the number
of rules of concord and government in any language
is dependent on the variety of its etymological inflections. (1861).

486. State the principal rules of English Syntax.
(1869).

487. Quote some rules of Concord in English
Syntax; and say how far the number of such rules
in any language is determined by the number and
variety of its grammatical inflections. (1870).

488. Give rules for the Agreement of Verbs and
Nominatives, and for the Sequence of Moods and
Tenses in the same sentence. (1868).

489. Point out and answer the chief questions
that may arise as to the application of the rule that
a Verb should agree with its Subject in Number
and Person. (1881).

490. What is meant by—"A verb agrees with
its subject in number and person"? Examine the
truth of the statement in English. (1878).

491. "The logical subject of a proposition is represented by the Nominative Case in Grammar."
Illustrate this statement, and point out, if you can,

E 2

any exceptions to it. Show also under what conditions the nominative in English is permitted to come *after* the verb. (1860).

492. In what number should you make the verb that is to agree with *news, ethics, riches, the odds, gentry, fish, firearms, tongs*? Give in each case your reason. (1863).

493. When the idea expressed by a noun is plural and the form singular, what is the number of the verb? Answer the same question when the idea is singular and the form plural. (1876).

494. Explain the concord of the following:— " The news is true " ; " The sheep are scattered"; "The Government are divided"; "Many are the blessings which intellectual and political freedom have brought in their train." (1865).

495. In what different ways are objective cases governed in English ? (1862).

496. Is there anything in English answering to an Absolute Case? If so, what case is it? Give examples. (1877).

497. Have we in English any idiom similar to the *Ablative absolute* in Latin? If so, explain it, and give examples of its use. (1863).

498. Some English grammarians say that the Absolute case in English is the Dative; others, that it is the Nominative. To which of these opinions do you incline? and on what grounds? (1866).

499. What is Apposition? Give some examples, and enunciate any rules which they respectively illustrate. (1873).

500. Why is it important which part of a compound word is placed first? (1861).

501. Illustrate by examples the points most worth attention in the Syntax of Pronouns. (1880).

502. Give the rules of Syntax which concern the use of Pronouns. (1872).

503. Give rules and examples showing the Syntax of the Pronoun, when it is either the subject or in any way related to the subject of a sentence. (1874).

504. Quote the rules for the concord and government of Relative Pronouns, and give examples. (1864).

505. Give some rule for determining the Case of a Relative Pronoun in an English sentence; and cite some examples. (1872).

506. Discuss the Etymology and Syntax of the Pronouns *who, what, which,* and *whether.* (1875).

507. Give examples of Correlative words in English, and some sentences illustrative of their proper use. (1871).

508. Write three short sentences showing the use of the word "that" (1) as a demonstrative pronoun, (2) as a relative pronoun, and (3) as a conjunction. (1874).

509. Give some rules which will be helpful in guarding against common errors in the use (1) of Relative Pronouns, (2) of "Shall" and "Will," (3) of the words "Than" and "As." (1871).

510. What verbs usually take respectively, (1) a dative, (2) a dative and accusative, and (3) a double accusative? What changes are involved in these constructions by the substitution of the Passive for the Active voice? (1876).

511. Distinguish between the Transitive and Intransitive Construction of a Verb, and give illustrations. Has every verb both? Compare these names with Active and Neuter. Point out the ordinary process by which a verb at first Transitive comes to be construed intransitively, and an Intransitive Verb comes to be used transitively. (1878).

512. Give rules for the right use of the Subjunctive in English, with examples. (1873).

513. When is a Subjunctive Mood used in English after such words as "if," "unless," &c. ? (1863).

514. Give three sentences in which the Subjunctive Mood is employed; and quote the rules which regulate its use. (1864).

515. "Duncan comes here to-night." Explain the use of the Present Indefinite in this sentence. What other distinct forms of thought can be expressed in English by the use of the same tense ? (1873).

516. Give some examples of the use of the Historical Present. (1872).

517. How are (1) Future and (2) Contingent events indicated in English ? State the rules, and construct examples in illustration. (1875).

518. State clearly the rules of English Syntax with regard to the use of *Will* and *Shall*. (1881).

519. What are the rules for the use of *shall* and *will* in Interrogative sentences? (1876).

520. What is the construction of English Impersonal verbs ? How do you account for the following in Milton ?—
"Him thought he by the brook of Cherith stood." (1875).

521. "Plain *living* and high thinking are no more"; "This *living* death." Distinguish grammatically between the two forms of the word italicised in these two sentences, and add some information about what is called the Infinitive Mood in Verbs. (1874).

522. Explain fully the various uses and constructions of *But, Than,* and *As,* respectively. (1867).

523. Write a few sentences to illustrate as fully

as you can the fact that the grammatical use of the same word may vary, so that it shall be now one part of speech and now another. (1874).

524. How is the absence of Case-endings supplied in English? State and illustrate the effect of this absence on the general structure of Sentences. Give examples of current words which retain traces of older Case-endings. (1869).

525. Paraphrase the following:—

Beauty—a living presence of the earth,
Surpassing the most fair ideal forms
Which craft of delicate spirits hath composed
From earth's materials—waits upon my steps :
Pitches her tent before me as I move,
An hourly neighbour. (1889).

526. Explain and give examples of the difference between Subordinate and Co-ordinate Sentences, between Extension and Completion of the Predicate, and between a Direct and an Indirect Object. (1881).

527. Define the meaning of the following grammatical terms, and give examples of their use:— "Relative " ; "Transitive " ; " Predicate "; " Infinitive " ; " Apposition." (1869).

528. Explain the terms Etymology, Syntax, Prosody, Declension, Case and the several names of Cases ; Gender; Conjugation, Mood, Tense ; Positive, Comparative, and Superlative. (1874).

529. Give examples of grammatical Pleonasm and Ellipsis in English. (1881).

530. Define Tautology, Verbiage, a Euphemism. (1882).

Correct or justify the following, giving your reason in every case:—

531. The Senate have decided.

532. The King with the Lords and Commons form the Legislature.

533. If thou beest he.

534. Whom do you think I am ?

535. From London to Brighton is fifty miles.

536. Did he not confess his fault, and begged to be forgiven ?

537. Our mutual friend.

538. I had hoped never to have seen the statues again.

539. Luckily the monks had recently given away a couple of dogs, which were returned to them, or the breed would have been lost.

540. It was the most amiable, although the least dignified, of all the party squabbles by which it had been preceded.

541. Having perceived the weakness of his poems, they now re-appear to us under new titles.

542. Neither you nor I am right.

543. I am one of those who cannot describe what I feel.

544. Whom they were, I really cannot specify.

545. His is a poem, one of the completest works that exists in any language.

546. He was shot at by a secretary under notice to quit, with whom he was finding fault—very fortunately without effect.

547. Who do you speak to ?

548. It was thought to be him.

549. The river has overflown its banks.

550. Let us make a covenant, I and thou.

551. None but the brave deserves the fair.

552. Whether or no I am right, you are certainly wrong.

553. They are both fond of one another.

554. Thersites body is as good as Ajax when neither are alive.

555. How much more elder art thou than thy looks.

556. The elder house.

557. There were no less than five persons concerned.

558. They are the six first lines in Paradise Lost.

559. Neither he nor we are disengaged.

560. One of the best books that has been written on the subject.

561. I like it better than any.

562. And since, I never dare to write as funny as I can.

563. Laying the suspicion upon somebody, I know not who, in the country.

564. Well is him that hath found prudence.

565. The threatened assault was met by Buckingham by a counter attack on the Earl of Bristol, whom he knew would be the chief witness against him.

566. They were desirous of removing those abuses which the Stewart Kings had introduced into the Government, and which overlaid the Constitution.

567.

"And many a holy text around she strews
That teach the rustic moralist to die."

568. This view has been maintained by one of the greatest writers that has appeared in this country.

569. The administration of so many various interests, and of districts so remote, demand no common capacity and vigour.

570. It has generally been observed that the European population of the United States is tall, and characterised by a pale and sallow countenance.

571. When distress and anguish cometh upon you.

572. By young Telemachus his blooming years.

573. Sorrow not as them that have no hope.

574. Breaking a constitution by the very same errors that so many have been broke before.

575. They are not only the most charitable of any other nation, but most judicious in distinguishing the properest objects of compassion.

576. The part of this reed used by the Indians is from ten to eleven feet long, and no tapering can be perceived, one end being as thick as another.

577. It is observable that each one of the letters bear date after his banishment.

578. If he had writ me word by the next post, this had been just and civil.

579. Regard is to be had to every one's circumstances, healths, and abilities.

580. He was neither learned in the languages nor philosophy.

581. I was going to have written him a letter.

582.
> " Now either spoke, as hope or fear impressed
> Each their alternate triumph in the breast."

583. The tale is to be in five chapters and I have finished the first three.

584.
> " No other river such fine salmon feed,
>   Nor Taff, nor Tay, nor Tyne, nor Thames, nor Trent,
>   nor Tweed."

585. You may take either of the nine.

586. Such are the difficulties with which the question is involved.

587. In depicting of characters, Werner is a mannerist.

588. The porch was the same width with the temple.

589. There is nobody but condemns this in others, though they overlook it in themselves.

590. Who can it be from?

591. In men, as in carriages, firmness and soft-

ness in each is the best arrangement for the safety of all.

592. The logical and historical analysis of a language often coincides.

593. A history now by a Mr. Hume would be examined with different eyes than had it borne any other name.

594. 'S cannot be a contraction of *his*, for it is put to *female nouns*.

595. *Men* are put in the plural number because they mean many.

596. It is neither Osmyn nor Jane Shore that speak.

597. His father's and his mother's names are on the blank leaf.

598. Like I did.

599. Their healths were drank with great enthusiasm.

600. Having failed in this attempt, no farther trial was made.

601. I am afraid you will be displeased with my meddling, which I should on no account have dared to do had not the alteration been small.

602. There are often a great variety of causes at work.

603. These people are no more reformers, and no more desire to make great changes, than did their ancestors.

604. Let each esteem other better than themselves.

605. The plan of publication between my friend and I was announced.

606. It is not me you are in love with.

607. We are still much at a loss who civil power belongs to.

608. The accounts they gave of the favourable reception of their writings with the public.

609. Government sometimes sells arms to whomsoever chooses to buy.

610. A subsequent edition has been published in 1822.

611. I prefer to leave a point untaught than to teach it in a way that must be unlearned.

612.

> " . . . . For the mind and spirit remains
> Invincible."

613. Few if any town or village in the South of England has a name ending in *by*.

614. The following facts may, or have been, adduced on the other side.

615. It is in such moments of gloom and despondency that the immortal superiority of genius and virtue most strongly appear.

616. I should prefer a verbal to a written message.

617. While shame, *thou looking on*, did utmost vigour raise. (*Milton*).

618. Homer as well as Vigil were studied on the banks of the Rhine. (*Gibbon*).

619. There is *sometimes more* than one auxiliary to a verb. (*Murray*).

620. *More than* a little is required of us. (*Butler*).

621. Nothing but grave and serious studies delight him.

622. Can England spare such men as him? (*Brougham*).

623. It is better for you and I as it is.

624. You ought *to have come*.

625. I expected *to have finished* at six.

626.

> "Mantua's law
> Is death to any he that utters them." (*Shakespeare*).

627. This sentence *of the Dean's* is itself ungrammatical. (*Cobbett*).

628. I could not see it in the posture I lay. (*Swift*).

629. You may infuse the sentiment by a ray of light, no thicker, nor one-thousandth part so thick, as the finest needle.

630. If he permits this, we shall speedily become as poor as them.

631. The books were lain upon the table by his direction.

632. Milton seems to have been well acquainted with his own genius, and to know what it was nature had bestowed on him.

633. Language is the principal vehicle of thought.

634. It laid upon a table as I entered.

635. They were cast and an heavy fine imposed upon them.

636. He called the Treasurer and Secretary, and they came in.

637. A number of them were drowned in the Lycus.

638. The number of the names were about an hundred and twenty.

639. Fair and softly goes far.

640. They are as follow.

641. I will communicate it with you.

642. His statement was very different to that.

643. How sweet the moonlight sleeps upon this bank.

644. Tell me in sadness whom is she you love.

645. You blame you know not who.

646. A year ago it was my purpose to have withdrawn my wealth to a safer country.

647. He was offered the command of the Baltic fleet.

648. The largest circulation of any liberal newspaper.

649. Injustice springs only from three causes. Neither of these causes for injustice can be found in a Being wise, powerful, and benevolent.

650. This dedication may serve almost for any book that has, is, or shall be published.

651. I meant to have written to you.

652. If I were old enough to be married, I am old enough to manage my husband's house.

653. In the best counties a rise in rents and wages has been found to go together.

654. He belongs to one caste, and the hewers of wood and drawers of water to another.

655. I heard of him running away.

656. It's me.

657. Swift, but a few months before, was willing to have hazarded all the horrors of a civil war.

658. Many a time.

659. All the better.

660. Between you and I, there is little hope that I will succeed.

661. A few hours of intercourse is enough for forming a judgment on the case.

662. To countenance persons who are guilty of bad actions is scarcely one remove from committing them.

663. His aversion from that case is strong.

664. All males are of the masculine gender.

665. Him excepted, all were lost.

666. He is not the man as told me the story.

667. That is not such a practice as I can sanction.

668. Thou lovest; but ne'er knew love's sad satiety.

669. Man never is but always to be blest.

670.

Macb. There's blood upon thy face.
Murd. 'Tis Banquo's then.
Macb. 'Tis better thee without than he within.

671.

"Like one
Who having unto truth, by telling of it,
Made such a sinner of his memory
To credit his own lie, he did believe
He was indeed the duke."

672.

"This is he, my master said,
Despised the Athenian Maid."

673. It is in such moments that the superiority of genius and virtue most strongly appear.

674. The richness of her arms and apparel were conspicuous in the foremost rank.

675. Neither Charles nor his brother were qualified to support such a system.

676. In every ward one of the King's council took every man's book, and sealed them, and brought them to Guildhall to confront them with the original.

677. You have bestowed your favours to the most deserving persons.

678. Upon such occasions as fell into their cognizance.

679. They accused the ministers for betraying the Dutch.

680. I dissent with the Examiner.

681. Policy prevails upon force.

682. The wisest princes need not think it any diminution to their greatness, or derogation to their sufficiency, to rely upon counsel.

683. Neither he nor I have any doubt of his success.

684. One of the best treatises that has ever been published.

685. I am one of those who cannot describe what I do not see.

686. The country was divided into counties, and the counties placed under magistrates.

687. Nobody ever put so much of themselves into their work.

688. He had given away above half his fortune to the Lord knows who.

689. Friendships which we once hoped and believed would never have grown cold.

690. Nepos answered him, Celsus replied, and neither of them were sparing of censures on each other.

691.

"The boy stood on the burning deck,
Whence all but he had fled."

692. Such are a few of the many paradoxes one could cite from his writings, and which are now before me.

693. I am verily a man who am a Jew.

694. Too great a variety of studies distract the mind.

695. Each shall be rewarded in their turn.

696. I knew it to be he.

697. Whom do you think he is ?

698. Neither our virtues or our vices are all our own.

699. That's him.

700. Many a day.

701. I expected to have found him better.

702. I am to blame.

703. He objects to me having the book.

704. One set of writers have looked merely to the letter of our statutes.

705. That is the man, whom I perceived, was in fault.

706. This is one of the best specimens of the kind that have ever fallen under our notice.

707. I never remember to have seen it before.

708. His haughtiness lost him all chance of success.

709. John deserved better, and was treated worse, than his brother is ever likely to be.

710. I never will, and never have, done it.

711. He told me that he would resume work to-day.

712. We might have placed A in one class with no more impropriety than we have placed B in the other.

713. It is most likely that neither of these are the correct version.

714. This man and that man was born there.

715. In modern English two negatives destroy one another.

716. Every one has their faults.

717. The admiration of this poem was unanimous.

718. The boats were drawn ashore, having first taken out the cargo.

719. He trusted to have equalled the Most High.

720. The Duke of Wellington is not one of those who interfere with matters over which he has no control.

721. We know little individually of his hearers.

722. It is quite true, what you say.

723. The other solution is more preferable.

724. We guarded Sir Roger to his lodging in the same manner that we brought him to the play-house.

725.

> What shall we say, since silent now is he
> Who, when he spoke, all things would silent be.

726. This announcement was a much greater blow to him than the former council was a support.

727. How different a |place looks when you are coming away from it to what it ever looked before !

F

723. You will soon find such peace which it is not in the power of the world to give.

729. He was no sooner out of the wood but he beheld a glorious scene.

730. Other geniuses I put in the second class; not as I think them inferior to the first, but for distinction's sake.

731. Many writers employ their wit in propagating of vice.

732. In proportion as either of these qualities [perspicuity and sublimity] are wanting, the language is imperfect. (*Addison*).

733. You have weakened instead of strengthened your case.

734. The Chinese laugh at European plantations, which are lain out by rule and line.

735. It bears some remote analogy with what I have described.

736. When we look at English Comedies, we would think that their authors do not care to brand the vices they describe.

737. You are in no danger of him.

738. Art thou proud yet?—Ay, that I am not thee.

739.
Whoever the king favours
The cardinal will find employment for.

740. Here you may see that visions are to dread.

741. Nothing but wailings was heard.

742. Neither of them are remarkable for precision.

743. I cannot tell if it be wise or no.

744. It must be confessed that a lampoon or a satire do not carry in them robbery and murder.

745.
Whose own example strengthens all his laws,
And is him elf the great Sublime he draws.

746. 'Tis they that still renew Ulysses' toils. (*Prior*).

747. The Duke of Wellington is one of those who never interferes with matters over which he has no control. (*Wellington*).

748. He is one of the wisest that has ever lived.

749. Neither the time nor the place of his birth are known with certainty. (*Robertson*).

750. It is hard to bear.

751. Whatever may be thought of the veracity of this story. (*Goldsmith*).

752. Who did you go with?

753.

" How beautiful must be
The God that made so great a thing as Thee ! "

754. We contributed a third more than the Dutch, who were obliged to the same proportion more than us. (*Swift*).

755. My paper is Ulysses his bow, in which every man of wit or learning may try his strength. (*Addison*).

756. But the temper as well as knowledge of a modern historian require a more sober and accurate language. (*Gibbon*).

757. He knows not what spleen, languor, or list-lessness are. (*Blair*).

758. This was in reality the easiest matter of the two. (*Shaftesbury*).

759. We need not, nor do not, confine the purposes of God. (*Bentley*).

760. If the king gives us leave, you or I may as lawfully preach as them that do. (*Hobbes*).

761. Nor is it then a welcome guest, affording only an uneasy sensation, and brings always with it a mixture of concern and compassion. (*Fielding*).

762. But the greatest error of all the rest is the

F 2

mistaking or misplacing of the last or furthest end
of knowledge. (*Bacon*).

763.

"Thou great first cause, least understood,
Who all my sense confined." (*Pope*).

764.

The sun has rose and gone to bed,
Just as if Partridge were not dead.   (*Swift*).

765. In the tempter of mind he was . . . (*Steele*).

766. . . . . which I had no sooner drank, but I
found a pimple rising in my forehead. (*Addison*).

767. 'Twas Love's mistake, who fancied what it
feared. (*Crabbe*).

768. Whom say ye that I am ?

769. From whence comes he ?

770. Whom the gods love die young.

771. O well is thee !

772. This principle is of all others the most important.

773. His conduct lost him the king's confidence.

774. He took his departure from the same point
from which his father had done.

775. He was angry at me quitting the house.

776. I had rather not go.

777. The king then entered on that career of
misgovernment, which, that he was able to pursue
it, is a disgrace to our history.

778.

Thy honourable metal may be wrought
From that it is disposed.

779.

What conscience dictates to be done,
Or warns me not to do,
This teach me more than hell to shun,
That, more than heaven pursue.

780. Whoe'er I woo, myself would be his wife.
(*Shakespeare*).

781. He would have spoke. (*Milton*).

782.
"O thou my voice inspire
Who touched Isaiah's hallow'd lips with fire." (*Pope*).

783.
" And though by Fate's severe decree
She suffers hourly more than me." (*Swift*).

784.
"For ever in this humble cell
L-t thee and I, my fair one, dwell." (*Prior*).

785. He is arrived.

786. The sight of his blood, whom they deemed invulnerable.

787. Nobody said so but him.

788. He had like to have been drowned.

789. The fact of me being a minor cannot matter.

790. He was scarce gone when you came.

791. He has eaten no food nor drunk no wine this two days.

792. Who should I meet to-day but him you are talking of.

793. Will that be all you want?

794. My " Lives of the Poets " are reprinting.

795. He or you are in the wrong.

796. Nor want nor cold his course delay.

797. What and if I did?

798. Every thought and feeling are opposed to it.

799. The Thames is derived from the Latin *Tamesis*.

800. Are either of these men your friend?

801. It is not me who he is in love with. ·

802. Who shall I give it to?

803. They will never believe but what I have been to blame.

804. Neither precept or discipline are so forcible as example.

805. The thunder was heard roll over our heads.

806. Men all slept sound save she who loved them both.

807. Extravagance as well as parsimony are to be avoided.

808. I am a man that have travelled and seen many nations. (*Steele*).

809. Impossible, it can't be me. (*Swift*).

810. And virgins smiled at what they blushed before. (*Pope*).

811. I have not wept this forty years. (*Dryden*).

812. If you were here, you would find three or four in the parlour after dinner, whom you would say passed their time very agreeably. (*Locke*).

813. The man neither knew the number of the coach, or recollected the coachman, or did he remember whither the coach was ordered to go. (*Charlotte Smith*).

814. Of all others he is the ablest writer they have.

815. There are many ways of dressing a calve's head.

816. You must either be quiet or must leave the room.

817. The Muses sung before the throne of Jupiter.

818. Thoughts are only criminal when they are first chosen and then voluntarily continued.

819. And when he was set he opened his mouth and taught.

820. You did not ought to go.

821. I called upon him, and wished to have submitted my MS. to him.

822. No man is so perfect but what he may err.

823. Methinks I see a mighty nation renewing her youth.

824. I had wrote to him the day before.

825. It was sang at the Philharmonic last year.

826. Ill would it fare with your lordship and I, if such a law should pass in Parliament.

827. Such a periodical as Arnold would have loved, and Coleridge promise to contribute to.

828. Scarves. Rooves. Moreover's. Court-Martials.

829. Virtuous conversation is a mean to work the heathen's conversion.

830. Be governed by your conscience, and never ask anybodies leave to be honest.

831. The posture of your blows are yet unknown.

832. A House to let.

833. They generally show marks who they come from.

834. A versifier and poet are two different things.

835. Liberal not lavish is kind Nature's hands.

836.

" Not Prester John or Cham of Tartary
Are in their houses monarch more than I."

837. I know how much pains have been taken in his case.

838. I wish to cultivate a farther acquaintance with you.

839. The sentence is faulty somewhat in the same manner with the last.

840. Myself is (not am) weak: Thyself is (not art) strong.

841. She fell a-laughing like one out of their right mind.

842. A wise man scorneth nothing, be it never so small or homely.

843. There are five compartments ; put it in either of them.

844.

> " Avoid extremes ; and shun the fault of such
> Who still are pleased too little or too much."

845. I was offered the post a year ago.

846. Gold, whose touch seductive leads to crime.

847. Of which doctrine we assert that no teaching can so certainly deaden spiritual life.

848. He sat him down on a pillar's base.

849. It is these that do the mischief.

850. I durst, my lord, to wager she is honest.

851. I reck not, so it light well aimed.

852. Either you or I is in the wrong.

853.

> . . . . Let us like Horace and Lydia agree ;
> For thou art a girl as much brighter than her
> As he was a poet sublimer than me.

854. Avoid those kind of things.

855. He printed a great number of authors in such a manner as show him to be a very ingenious and learned man.

856. *Petulant* —You were the quarrel.
Millamant.—Me !

857. His worship and strength is in the clouds.

858. Neither Charles nor William were there.

859. Good order and not mean savings produce great profit.

860. The two first boys in the class.

861. Alfred, than whom never wiser prince governed England.

862. Whether you will or no.

863. He does not know but what it is true.

864. Are either of those horses yours ?

865. He went away all of a sudden.

866. It was thought to be he.

867. In 1829 Mr. Froude or Mr. R. Wilberforce or Mr. Newman were but individuals.

868. It is good sort of people who are tempted to it.

869. This impatience and repining is natural to the young.

870. The execution may be as gradual as is found convenient.

871. There was not a philosopher's door but opened to him of its own accord.

872. We can easier descend than ascend.

873. Whom do you suppose called on me to-day?

874. Without you learn it soon it will be too late.

875. He ordered no one to leave the room.

876. What kind of an article is *the*?

877. These ten last examples are of a different nature to the former.

878. Seldom or ever did a lawyer rise to eminence by wit.

879. Wrongs are engraved on marble, benefits too often on sand: these are apt to be requited, those forgot.

880. They drowned the black and white kittens. Thinking of them, my pen tarries as I write. The then Ministry. I intended to have written to him.

881. Criticise the grammar or style of the following:—

(*a*) It is characteristic of them to appear but to one person, and he the most likely to be deluded.

(*b*) I think it may assist the reader by placing them before him in chronological order.

(*c*) Few people learn anything that is worth learning easily.

(*d*) My resolution is to spare no expense in education; it is a bad calculation, because it is the only advantage over which circumstances have no control.

(*e*) Image after image, phrase after phrase,

starts out vivid, harsh, and emphatic. (1886).

882. Criticise and correct the following pieces of grammar and style :—

(a) Books that we can at a glance carry off all that is in them are worse than useless for discipline.

(b) He preferred to know the worst than to dream the best.

(c) Humanity seldom or ever shows itself in inferior dispositions.

(d) You have already been informed of the sale of Ford's theatre, where Mr. Lincoln was assassinated, for religious purposes.

(e) The Moor seizing a bolster, full of rage and jealousy, smothers her.

(f) Nor do I know any one with whom I can converse more pleasantly, or I would prefer as my companion. (1887).

883. What is meant by an "idiom"? Mention two or three English idioms, and try to explain them. (1886).

884. Point out what is idiomatic in these phrases: "There came a letter." "Let them fight it out." "We spoke to each other." "Many a man would flee." "What an angel of a girl!" "What with this, and what with that, I could not get on." (1886).

885. Give the sources of the following expressions, pointing out the objection to their use as English idioms, and showing how the meaning might in each case be properly conveyed:—

The window gives upon the street.
That goes without saying.
That affair came upon the carpet.
He is feeble as to his mind.

Solidarity of interests.
A new standpoint.
He affected the latest fashion.
They were elected upon the same platform.
To exploit this new invention.
To mediatize.
Interpellation. (1888).

886. Explain the following constructions:—"Is the news true?" "The people are divided." "Every limb and every feature appears with its appropriate grace." "Justice, as well as benevolence, is our rule."

887. Explain the syntax of the following sentences, with special reference to the words *italicised* :—

He was paid a *shilling*. I taught him *Latin*. He walked twenty *miles*. That is a horse of *mine*. It grieves me to hear this. *Who* runs may read.

> "There is no man here
> *But* honours you." (1871).

838. What exactly is meant by the term "parse"? (1883).

889. Parse the word *what* in the sentences —
I will tell you *what*.
He was some*what* weary.
What o'clock is it?
What man is this?
What with the wind, and what with the rain, it was not easy to get on. (1884).

890. Parse these sentences—
(1) The Lord hear thee in the day of trouble.
(2) They gave him such a reception as gratified him, and such an answer as he wished to receive. (1868).

891. Parse all the words ending in *ing* in this sentence :—" Darkling, we went singing on our way,

with our walking-sticks in our hands, weary of toil-
ing in town." (1884).

892. Parse *must* in " He says he *must* go," and
"He said he *must* go "; and mention some other
verbs that are similarly unchanged. (1887).

893. Parse the *italicised* words and phrases :—

(a) *Down* with it !

(b) His *having been beaten* once only made him
the more determined to succeed.

(c) *Seeing* is *believing.*

(d) The *hearing* ear and the *seeing* eye, the
Lord hath made *even* both of them.

(e) *Whatever* sceptic could inquire for,
For every *why* he had a *wherefore.*

(f) *Let* knowledge *grow* from *more* to more.
(1887).

894.

"The curfew tolls the knell cf parting day."

" . . . Parting is such sweet sorrow
That I shall say Good night till it be morrow."

First parse and then analyse each of these sentences. Explain, with reference to earlier forms of
inflection, the two grammatical uses of the word
you find in both of them. (1871).

895. Say to what part of speech each of the
italicised words belong, and give your reasons:—
" He told me *that* I was wanted." " They will all
come *but* him." " *Where* the bee sucks, *there* lurk
I." " How *do* you do? " " How *sweet* the moonlight sleeps upon this bank ! " (1864).

896. Give instances in which the same word may
be either

Noun, Adjective, or Verb ;

Noun, Adjective, or Adverb ;

Verb, Adjective, or Adverb ;

Adverb, Preposition, or Conjunction ;

Adjective, Adverb, or Preposition ;

Pronoun, Adverb, or Conjunction. Was this always so? If not, how has it arisen? (1878).

897. Enumerate and distinguish the various meanings and uses of the word *but*. (1876).

898. Parse each of the four words, "But me no buts." What other parts of speech may "but" be? Would you say "They all ran away but me," or "They all ran away but I"? (1886).

899. Discuss the form *Methinks*. (1868).

900. Distinguish between "I think" and "Me-thinks." What is the grammatical structure of each of the following phrases?—" The self-same day;" "Many a day;" "A house to let;" "Lady-day;" "To wit;" By rights;" "Forty pounds a year;" "A few things." (1873).

901. Discuss the force of the termination *-ing* in the following sentences:—

(1) Plain liv*ing* and high think*ing* are no more.
(2) The enemy took to runn*ing*.
(3) He is com*ing*.
(4) They are gone a-fish*ing*.
(5) The house is a-build*ing*. (1875).

902. Explain the precise signification of the words *it* and *there* in the sentences:—It rains; It is he; I struck it with a sword; There lived a man; Are there many in the room? There, at the foot of yonder nodding beech; Go there as fast as possible; Is it not we that are in fault? (1873).

903. Account for "his" in the following pas-sage:—If the salt have lost *his* savour." (1865).

904. Is it correct to speak of "a two-foot rule"? (1883).

905. Parse—

Bolingbroke.—Good Aunt, stand up.
Duchess of York.—   I do not sue to stand,
     Pardon is all the suit I have in hand.

Bolingbroke.—I pardon him, as God shall pardon me
Duchess.—O happy vantage of a kneeling knee !
      Yet am I sick for fear : speak it again ;
      Twice saying pardon does not pardon twain,
      But makes one pardon strong. (1875).

906. Parse *after* in each of the following sentences:—"His *after* life shows him to greater advantage;" " *after* him then and bring him back; "
" *after* he came all went wrong;" "you go first and
I will come *after*;" " *after* that I will say no more;"
—and *out* in " *out* brief candle;" " he was quite *out*
of it;" " *out* upon it;" "he was beaten *out* and
out;" " he proved an *out* and *out* deceiver." (1885).

907. Explain the forms in italics:—"The time is
com*en* wh*aune* trew*e* worshipers *schuln* worship the
fa*dir* in spirit and truth*e*. God is a spirit, and it
behoveth *hem* that worship*en*, so to worship*an*
hym." (1860).

908. In what cases are the several words italicised?—This cost five *shillings*. He was offered a
pension. He died as a *Christian*. He lived a *saint*.
"And all the *air* a solemn *stillness* holds." The in-
vestment yielded *me* large profit. (1869).

909. What designations would you give to the
cases severally employed in the following?—

(*a*) Be *of good cheer.*
(*b*) Take a glass *of wine.*
(*c*) *All things considered*, I am glad.
(*d*) He *did the deed.* (1882).

910. Explain the italicised words in each of these
sentences:—"How *do* you *do?* "

        " And every shepherd *tells* his *tale*
        Under the hawthorn in the dale." (1872).

911. Discuss the words italicised in the following:—

SYNTAX. 79

" Long *ago* we were *wont* to let plain *living* accompany high *thinking*."

"*Methinks* you *might* have spoken, but you *durst* not." (1881).

912. Discuss these phrases :—

(*a*) He found them *fled*, horses *and all*.

(*b*) Fight *away*, my men.

(*c*) *Get you gone*.

(*d*) I give you this *to boot*.

(*e*) *To oversleep myself*.

(*f*) How did he *come by* such a fortune ? (1887).

913. After what verbs is *to* generally not inserted before the infinitive ? (1865.)

914. What is *to* in the following expressions ?— " Early *to* bed and early *to* rise ; " " Go *to* now ; " " And all *to* break his head ; " " Such a *to*-do ; " " *To*-day ; " " What went ye out for *to* see ?" (1865, 1869, 1876).

915. Parse the following vocables :—*Alms* ; *Valuables* ; *Riches* ; *Mews* ; *Greens* ; *Kine*. (1867).

916. Parse the sentence—

" He that is down need fear no fall,
He that is low, no pride." (1872).

917. Explain and parse the following phrases :— *Methinks* ; *woe is me* ; *I was an hungered* ; *I had as lief*. (1885).

918. Parse :—

(*a*) Murder will out.

(*b*) Mark but my fall and that that ruined me.

(*c*) Love such things as are of good report. (1865).

919. Parse the sentence—

" Were I Brutus,
And Brutus Antony, there were an Antony
Would ruffle up your spirits." (1864).

920. Point out the grammatical difference between *the* in such a phrase as "he did his duty, and was the happier for it," and the *the* in "he was the happier of them." (1883).

921. Classify the words *pen, petition, long, that wire.* (1883).

X. ANALYSIS.

922. Define a Sentence, a Phrase, and a Clause, and give instances of each. (1835, 1839).

923. Define a Sentence ; and state what is meant by a Noun clause, an Adjective clause, and an Adverbial clause. Give an example of each. (1865).

924. What is the use of the "analysis of sentences"? What shapes may the subject of a sentence assume? And in what ways may it be extended? (1886).

925. What does Analysis mean? State and explain the various terms employed in the analysis of sentences. (1877).

926. Give some general directions for the Analysis of Sentences, and apply them to a sentence of your own composing. (1885, 1887, 1888).

927. What are the necessary elements in every sentence? Show by examples some different ways in which a simple sentence may be expanded and rendered complex. (1872).

928. Define Subject, Predicate, and Copula. What is the difference between the Logical and the Grammatical division of a Proposition? (1868.)

929. Into what two parts may every Simple or Complex Sentence be divided. How many enlargements and extensions does each part admit? (1868).

930. Explain fully the mode of analysing Complex sentences. (1866).

931. Give examples showing how the predicate of a sentence may be modified (1) by a Word,

G

(2) by a Phrase, (3) by a subordinate Sentence. (1871).

932. Give examples of sentences in which the predicate is enlarged (*a*) by an adjunct, (*b*) by a subordinate sentence. Parse either grammatically or logically the passage—

> "If Virtue feeble were,
> Heaven itself would stoop to her." (1863).

933. Write a sentence containing three extensions of the predicate, one of them a clause, and let this clause contain a subject with two extensions. (1886).

934. In what various ways may the Subject of a sentence be enlarged? In what the Predicate extended? Compose a sentence to illustrate your answers. (1887).

935. What is an Attribute? Specify all the kinds of attributes which a substantive may have, with examples. Can you have an attribute of an attribute? (1878).

936. Define the terms "inflection;" "analysis;" "synthetic;" "interjection;" "strong" and "weak" as applied to verbs; "abstract" and "concrete," as applied to nouns; "simple" and "complex," as applied to sentences. (1885).

937. Make a sentence containing a simple subject and predicate only; and add other sentences showing how subject or predicate may be enlarged by phrases or by subordinate sentences. Resolve the following sentence into its elements:—

> "What seem'd his head
> The likeness of a kingly crown had on." (1864).

938. Divide the following verse into separate sentences, and say how they are related to one

another, and what is the subject and predicate in each : parse the words *italicised* :

"Blow, *blow* thou winter *wind* !
    Thou art not so unkind
      As man's *ingratitude* :
    Thy tooth is not *so* keen !
    Because thou *art* not *seen*,
      Although thy breath *be* rude." (1871).

939. Place each of the following phrases in a sentence of your own construction, so as to illustrate the way in which it may be properly used :— Better than he ; Better than him ; Than whom ; And which ; As good as I ; As good as me ; The wiser man ; Would that ; Sixty head. (1870).

940. Put the following phrases into sentences ; and give a reason for the construction which you employ :—
"As good as I." "As good as me." "Wiser than he." "Wiser than him." "Than whom." "A friend of my brother's." "All but her." "Many a man." "You and I." "You and me." (1864).

941. Analyse the following sentences :—

" But me, not destined such delights to share,
My prime of life in wandering spent and care ;
Impelled with steps unceasing to pursue
Some fleeting good that mocks me with the view ;
That like the circle bounding earth and skies
Allures from far, yet, as I follow, flies ;
My fortune leads to traverse realms alone,
And find no spot of all the world my own."

942. We reckon more than five months yet to harvest ; there need not be five weeks ; had we but eyes to lift up, the fields are white already. Where there is much desire to learn, there of necessity will be much arguing, much writing, many opinions ;

for opinion in good men is but knowledge in the
making.

943. What is this?

944. I had rather not go.

945. Who is he to behave in such a manner?

946. There were leaders in multitudes ; but their
money went for other purposes, as their admiration
was fixed elsewhere.

947. His answers were such as to win unqualified
praise.

948. I am monarch of all I survey.

949. 'Tis love that makes the world go round.

950. His business was to beat the enemy, and he
knew he could not beat the enemy unless he could
get the best officers it was possible to get.

951. There is no branch of human work whose
constant laws have not close analogy with those
which govern every other mode of man's exertion.

952.
> " But knowledge to their eves her ample page
> Rich with the spoils of time did ne'er unfold."

953. Swift would say—" The thing has not life
enough to keep it sweet."

Johnson—" The creature possesses not vitality
sufficient to preserve it from putrefaction."

954.
> " Fame is the spur that the clear spirit doth raise,
> That last infirmity of noble mind,
> To scorn delights and live laborious days ;
> But the fair guerdon when we hope to find,
> And think to burst out into sudden blaze,
> Comes the blind Fury with the abhorred shears
> And slits the thin-spun life."

955. He that goeth about to persuade a multitude
that they are not so well governed as they ought to
be, shall never want attentive and favourable
hearers : because they know the manifold defects
whereunto every kind of regiment is subject; but

the secret lets and difficulties which in public proceedings are inevitable, they have not the judgment
to consider. (*Hooker*).

956.

> " There is a tide in the affairs of men
> Which, taken at the flood, leads on to fortune ;
> Omitted, all the voyage of their life
> Is bound in shallows and in miseries."

957. Would you know whether the tendency of
a book is good or evil, examine in what state of
mind you lay it down.

958.

> " My way of life
> Is fall'n into the sear, the yellow leaf ;
> And that which should accompany old age,
> As honour, love, obedience, troops of friends,
> I must not look to have."

959. I was confirmed in this opinion, that he,
who would not be frustrate of his hope to write
well hereafter in laudable things, ought himself to
be a true poem.

960.

> " What thou biddest,
> Unargued I obey."

961.

> " The dead man's knell
> Is there scarce asked for who ; and good men's lives
> Expire before the flowers in their cups,
> Dying or ere they sicken."

962.

> " The noble horse,
> That in his fiery youth from his wide nostrils
> Neighed courage to his rider, bearing his lord
> Safe to triumphant victory, old or wounded,
> Was set at liberty and freed from service."

963.

> "This day, to-morrow, yesterday, alike
> I am, I shall be, have been, in my mind
> Towards thee ; towards thy silence as thy speech."

964. A step was taken this session which was important in as far as it tended to separate the idea of death-punishment from crimes which were no longer capital.

965. By our common law, although there be for the prince provided many princely prerogatives and royalties, yet it is not such as the prince can take money or other things, or do as he will at his own pleasure, without order, but quietly to suffer his subjects to enjoy their own, without wrongful oppression : wherein other princes by their liberty do take as pleaseth them.

966. Rab I saw almost every week on the Wednesday; and we had much pleasant intimacy. I found the way to his heart by frequent scratching of his huge head, and an occasional bone. When I did not notice him he would plant himself straight before me and stand wagging that bud of a tail and looking up, with his head a little to one side.

967. I shall begin with that which, though the least in consequence, makes perhaps the most impression on our senses, because it meets our eyes in our daily walks,—I mean our retail trade. The exuberant display of wealth in our shops was the sight which most amazed a learned foreigner of distinction who lately resided among us. His expression, I remember, was, that "they seemed to be bursting with opulence into the streets."

968. What other excellences this garden of Paradise had, before God for man's ingratitude and cruelty cursed the earth, we cannot judge ; but I may safely think that by how much Adam exceeded all living men in perfection, by being the immediate workmanship of God, by so much did that chosen and particular garden exceed all parts of the universal world, in which God had planted, that is, made to grow, the trees of life, of knowledge ; plants

only proper and becoming the paradise and garden
of so great a Lord.

969. We fear by light as children in the dark.

970.

"Yet e'en these bones from insult to protect,
Some frail memorial still erected nigh,
With uncouth rhymes and shapeless sculpture decked,
Implores the passing tribute of a sigh.

Their name, their years, spelt by th' unletter'd Muse,
The place of fame and elegy supply ;
And many a holy text around she strews
That teach the rustic moralist to die.

For who to dumb forgetfulness a prey,
This pleasing anxious being e'er resigned,
Left the warm precincts of the cheerful day,
Nor cast one longing lingering look behind ? "

971. The world beheld with astonishment two
Princes, whose rival pretensions had for so many
years distracted Europe with divisions and deluged
it with blood, now suddenly bound together by the
closest ties of alliance.

972.

" It little profits that, an idle king,
By this still hearth, among these barren crags,
Matched with an aged wife, I mete and dole
Unequal laws unto a savage race,
That hoard, and sleep, and feed, and know not me.''

973.

This sea that bares her bosom to the moon,
The winds that will be howling at all hours,
And are upgather'd now like sleeping flowers,
For this, for everything, we are out of tune.

974. In the olden days, in which distance could
not be vanquished without toil but in which the
toil was rewarded, there were few moments of which
the recollection was more fondly cherished by the
traveller than that which brought him within sight of

Venice. Not but that the aspect of the city itself was generally the source of some slight disappointment.

975.

> Of man's first disobedience, and the fruit
> Of that forbidden tree whose mortal taste
> Brought death into the world, and all our woe,
> With loss of Eden, till one greater Man
> Restore us, and regain the blissful seat
> Sing, Heavenly Muse.

976. I saw them run.

977. He can make it go.

978. Let her depart.

979. Who is it?

980. He was crowned king.

981. He was hanged—a well-deserved punishment.

982. Who was happier than Rolf when abroad on his skiff on one of the most glorious days of the year? He found his angling tolerably successful near home; but the further he went the more the herrings abounded; and he therefore dropped down the fiord with the tide, fishing as he receded, till all home subjects had disappeared.

983.

> What thou art, we know not;
>   What is most like thee?
> From rainbow clouds there flow not,
>   Drops so bright to see,
> As from thy presence showers a rain of melody.

984.

>   Gradual sinks the breeze
> Into a perfect calm, that not a breath
> Is heard to quiver through the closing woods,
> Or rustling turn the many twinkling leaves
> Of aspen tall.

985.

> O what a tangled web we weave,
> When first we practise to deceive!

986.
> She sat like patience on a monument,
> Smiling at grief.

987.
> And statesmen of her Council met
> Who knew the seasons, when to take
> Occasion by the hand, and make
> The bounds of freedom wider yet.

938. Give rules for Punctuation, and frame a sentence showing, by subordinate clauses, the use of the comma, semicolon, and colon. (1862, 1882, 1838, 1889).

XI. Derivation.

989. Define a Root; an English Root. What are Hybrids? Mention any Hybrids that are generally recognised as good English. (1882).

990. Explain the following terms applied to the structure of words:—*root, stem, primary derivative, secondary derivative, compound word.* Apply your explanation to the words *song, bait, batch, seeds, thicket, spider, farthing, landscape, knowledge, wedlock, hemlock, eyry, along, gossip, waylay, walkingstick.* (1880).

991. What is meant by *English Roots?* What letter-changes from the English root have occurred in the following words:—*each, thunder, speak, crumb?* (1881).

992. How are compounds and derivatives distinguished? How is hybridism in composition avoided? (1863).

993. What is meant by Diminutives and Augmentatives? Enumerate and illustrate by examples the suffixes most commonly used in English in the formation of such words, and of Patronymics. (1882).

994. Explain the formation of Diminutives in the English language, and give examples. (1858).

995. Give some examples in English of Compound words. How may such words be classified? (1864).

996. Classify Compound words in English, and give examples. (1877).

997. Distinguish Compound and Derivative words. (1865).

998. Enumerate, and explain the origin of, the various kinds of suffixes employed in the formation of English Ordinals. Give the etymology of *Foremost*. (1881).

999. Distinguish between the terms "cognate" and "derived" as applied to words. Mention some words cognate with *bear* (the verb), and some derived from it. (1885).

1000. What is the difference between a Root and a Derivative? Illustrate your answer by a comment on the history or form of these words:—*seam*; *ditch*; *weft*; *bishop*; *proof*; *ought*; *receive*; *went*; *mistress*. (1870).

1001. Make a list of the most common Nounformatives, with instances of their use and explanations of their force or forces. (1885).

1002. "Words indicating relations are often traceable to nouns and verbs." Comment on this statement, and illustrate it by examples. (1870).

1003. Trace the derivation of the words *strength, wrought, weft, wealth, uncouth, songstress, twain, drench, methinks, ought, vixen, farthing*. (1872).

1004. Derive *score, dozen, hundred, eleven*. How are distributive Numerals expressed in English? Give the first three English ordinal adverbs. (1882).

1005. Mrs. Quickly reports to Prince Henry that Falstaff "said this other day, you *ought* him a thousand pound." Explain that use of the word *ought*; show how we come by the two forms *own* and *owe*; account also for the forms *durst, quoth*, and *methinks*. (1883).

1006. Explain each part of the following words :—
re-n-d-er, dam-s-el, neg-oci-able, wand-er, spect-ac-le-s, slug-g-ish, cors-l-et, s-queam-ish, dec-ade, de-cad-ence, doom's-day, domin-ion, dom-est-ic. (1863).

1007. Give explanations of the following forms and words:—*sea-m, ru-th-less, e-spouse, mead-ow, aur-ic-ul-ar, Leon-ard, ducat, cravat, fir-st, un-aware-s, y-clad, who-m, did, n-ei-ther, in-m-ost.*

That *Mediterranean* City, Coventry. (*Holland*).

The frigid zone is *inhabitable* for extremitie of cold. (*Sandys*).

For this night *shaltou deyen* for my sake. (*Chaucer*). (1862).

1008. Comment on the derivation and structure of the following words, and state whether it is right to consider any of them as anomalous or exceptional in form:—*kine; spinster; shepherdess; reliable; unjust; mineralogy; its; deodorise; children; sovereign; himself; honour; talkative.* (1861).

1009. Explain the formation of the words *dean, sexton, vinegar, biscuit, tile, orchard, livelihood, allow, isle, island,* and add a few comments upon the phonetic changes illustrated by their history. (1882).

1010. With what familiar English words are the following derivatives connected?—*ditch; ought; wander; should; gift; month; husband; doomsday; length; woof; huntsman; seed; burden; forlorn; shadow; mirth.* (1864).

1011. Tell what you know of the history of the words, *aye, yea, yes, no, nay.* Explain how you would classify them among Parts of Speech. (1883).

1012. Comment on the following, their spelling, accent, or etymology:—*pigmy, sovereign, mobocracy, Grimsby, Manchester, Lincoln, jovial, hermetic, neck-handkerchief, essay, nature.* (1868).

1013. Give the etymology of the following words:—*monarch, somnambulist, immature, immaculate, manuscript, mendacious, participle, amputate, anarchy, epithet, synonymous.* (1858).

1014. What do you know of the origin of these words ?—*College* ; *University* ; *degree* ; *examine* ; *student* ; *scholar* ; *pass* ; *fail* ; *list* ; *matriculate*. (1885).

1015. What are the derivations of *dunce, copper, tramway, gipsy* ? (1881).

1016. Give the derivation, and explain the meaning, of the terms :—*Grammar, Alphabet, Noun, Neuter, Participle, Plural, Vowel, Diphthong, Apposition*. (1878).

1017. What affixes are used in English to express diminutiveness, (*a*) in nouns, (*b*) in adjectives, and (*c*) in verbs ? Give affixes that indicate an agent, a state, and a place. (1862).

1018. Show by what prefixes or terminations you can recognise

(1) Adjectives derived from nouns ;
(2) Nouns derived from adjectives ;
(3) Verbs derived from nouns or adjectives ;
(4) Adverbs derived from pronouns. (1863).

1019. Explain the origin of the suffixes in the following words :—*shadow, hillock, holy, busy, farthing, darling, worship, favour, burgess, ceremony, enemy, homage, terrace*. (1885).

1020. Name six prefixes and a dozen affixes of *Saxon* origin, and explain the force of each. Name six prefixes and six affixes of *Classic* origin. (1859).

1021. Write a list of the chief Teutonic Suffixes used in forming English Nouns, and tell what you can of the origin of each of them. (1873).

1022. Explain the origin and force of the terminations *-fy, -ize, -ty, -head, -th, -est, -ness* ; and give illustrations showing to what Part of Speech words having these endings respectively belong. (1871).

1023. Tell what you know of the origin of each

of the following suffixes:— *-er, -ness, -dom, -hood, -lock, -red, -ship, -ery, -et, -let, -age,* and *-tion.* (1874).

1024. Trace the history, and discriminate the uses, of the termination *-ing.* (1877).

1025. Give English prefixes and suffixes of Latin and Greek origin answering to the following of Saxon origin :—*Al-*mighty, *ill-*starred, *thorough-*fare, *with-*stand, clean-*se,* wood-*en,* black-*en,* glow-*ing,* learn-*ed.* (1861).

1026. Give one example of each form of the derivation of Nouns from other nouns, from adjectives, and from verbs by the use of suffixes. (1875).

1027. Give the exact force of the following prefixes and affixes : — man*hood*; spin*ster*; weft; seam ; slav*ish* ; tire*some*; spark*le*; *mis*give ; *for*get; *with*stand; betroth; *in*nocent; never. (1867).

1028. What do you know of words terminating as follows, (1) as to the part of speech to which they belong, (2) as to the language from which they are derived?—*-ful*; *-ize*; *-en*; *-ible*; *-ness*; *-ty*; *-ous*; *-ar*; *-ory*; *-tion*; *-fy*; *-ling*; *-less*; *-isk.* (1864).

1029. State the force or forces of the suffixes : *-ster, -ism, -let, -some, -ard, -ish.* Mention three prefixes of Teutonic origin and three of Romanic. (1886).

1030. Explain the suffixes in the following words:—*kingdom, every, seemly, business, farthing, hardship, piecemeal, nostril, gospel, orchard, namesake.* (1888).

1031. What ideas are indicated by the following prefixes and suffixes ?—ey-*ry,* bant-*ling,* part-*ic-le,* wit-*ness,* trump-*et,* tromb-*one,* win-*some,* s-patter, *c-*rumple, *un-*done, *a-*board, *a-*hungry. (1861).

1032. State the origin and describe the force of the following prefixes and suffixes respectively :— *re-, -ness, -kin, -for, -tion, dis-, -our, pre-, -ster, sub-, pur-, -ful.* (1869).

1033. What is the force of *-en* and *-er*, as terminations,—in nouns, in adjectives, and in verbs? (1870).

1034. Explain the suffixes in the words *hillock, hemlock, wedlock, knowledge, freedom, fellowship* ; and account for the vowel in the first syllable of the words *kitten, vixen, thimble.* (1872).

1035. Classify the principal Suffixes of the English language, (1) according to their origin; (2) according to their significance. (1877).

1036. What are our commonest Adjective formatives? (1887).

1037. By the help of Suffixes, convert the following Adjectives into Nouns :—

sweet; humble; wise; broad; pure; perfect; and the following nouns into adjectives :—

snow; grace; brother; sense; fool; wood;

Give two other examples of each formation; and state to what language each suffix belongs. (1869).

1038. Take the following Adjectives and convert them, by the help of prefixes or suffixes, into Verbs :—

large, just, humble, strong, wide;

and take the following verbs and convert them into Nouns :—

sow, sew, dig, weave, compel, receive, think.

Explain in each case the law of formation, and give other examples of it. (1873).

1039. Give some account of our Teutonic Noun-suffixes. (1882).

1040. Write out a list of prefixes, distinguishing those of English from those of Latin origin. Cite some examples of Hybridism in English words. (1870).

1041. Explain the meaning of the following suffixes, and state from what languages they are derived:—*-fy, -ness, -tion, -ible, -en, -isk, -ly, -tude.* (1860).

1042. Give the exact meaning of the following prefixes and suffixes:—*for*lorn, *mis*use, *ab*stract, *op*pose, *be*speak, liveli*hood*, whit*en*, wood*en*, black*ish*, satch*el*, haw*kin*. (1860).

1043. Explain the meaning of the following suffixes:— *-dom, -hood, -th* or *-t, -ard, -ee, -age*, and give three examples of each. (1858).

1044. Account for suffix or inflection in each of the following words:—*chicken, oxen, vixen, beeves, pennies, pence, spinster, widower, gander, drake.* (1883).

1045. Account for the letters printed in italics in scent, co*ll*e*ague*, fit*t*ed, foo*l*, i*s*land, ma*d*e, symbol, num*b*er. (1859).

1046. Explain the following forms, and state in each case the meaning of the italicised letters:— poet-*ess*, weal-*th*, dast-*ard*, satch-*el*, man-*hood*, *with*-stand, *for*-give, blu-*ster*, *be*-dim, *be*-times, truth-*ful*, John-*son*, cou-*l*-d, *to*-morro*w*. (1865).

1047. Account for the part in italics in each of the following words, and show its meaning and use:—duch*ess*; hi*m*; the*irs*; smel*ted*; swi*ne*; rever*end*; grew; m*ight*; wo*uld*; d*urst*; bet*ter*. (1863).

1048. Account for the presence of the italicised letters in the following words:—*i*mpossible, num*b*er; tend*er*; night*in*gale; pai*r*; rec*ei*ve; deb*t*; hono*u*r; civili*s*ation (compare " civilize ") ; refer-*r*ing; *c*hemistry; inflam*m*ation (compare " in-flame ") ; the Mar*y*s. (1870).

1049. Account for the letters in italics in *r*am*e* ;

these; those; passe*n*ger; sovere*ig*n; wet*t*est; ci*t*ies; potato*es*; sceptre; sceptic; hand*i*work; righteous; tom*b*; cou*l*d; o*u*r. (1879).

1050. Account for the italicised portions of the following words:—*ne*wt; cow*ard*; stream*let*; asleep; enough; *at*onement; kin*d*red; *gain*say; *f*orgive; a*m*; lov*eth*. (1876).

1051. Explain the presence of the italicised letters in the following words:—s*c*ent; *c*hamber; lo*d*ge; pla*gu*e; co*a*st; can*n*on; cou*l*d. (1867).

1052. Trace the derivation of the words *stitch, rouse, wrench, dole, loss, loan, sud, glaze, dredge,*—distinguishing between primary and secondary derivatives. (1874).

1053. Show that the following words were originally compound nouns:—*barn, orchard, stirrup.* Tell what you know of the Teutonic suffixes used in the forming of abstract nouns. (1883).

1054. How are English Compounds known, in print and pronunciation? Which is the defining word in compounds? Comment on the following:—A Finger-ring, a Well-head, a Tell-tale. (1870).

1055. Give some examples of Norman-French words in English; say what are their general characteristics as to meaning, and how far they are recognisable by their form. (1873).

1056. Take the forms *man, fer (fero),* and *graph (grapho)*; add as many prefixes and affixes as you can, giving the force of each. (1868).

1057. Why does the addition of *en* change the word *cat* into *kitten*? (1873).

1058. Distinguish etymologically between *sensitive* and *sensible*; *ye* and *you*; *confess* and *profess*; *verity* and *veracity*; *tense* and *time*; *ingenious* and *ingenuous*; *swear* and *forswear*; *seem* and *beseem.* (1872).

H

1059. Addison wrote in the Spectator, "The men begun to embellish themselves." Comment on this with reference to the origin and history of such forms as *began* and *begun*, *rang* and *rung*. (1872).

1060. Make a comment on the form or history of the words — *princess, each, sovereign, neither, hindmost, sempstress, what, went, ought, himself.* (1871).

1061. Discuss the propriety of such forms as "Moneyed," "Comfortable," "Positivist," "Telegram," "Bicycle." (1869).

1062. Point out anything faulty or objectionable in the composition of these words :—*witticism, streamlet, height, unreverend, huntress, he-goat, fertilise, Anti-State-Church, pureness.* (1872).

1063. State what you know of the Etymology of the following words:—*blame; pay; not; wig; miscreant; stipulation; rigmarole; renegade; twelve; such.* (1877).

1064. Explain how it is that we have such forms as *Sunday* and *Monday* alongside of such forms as *Wednesday* and *Thursday.* Also, how is it we say *Lady-day* and not *Lady's-day?* (1884).

1065. Show that *foremost* is a double superlative; *children* a double plural, *songstress* a double feminine; and give other examples of such doublings. (1884).

1066. Discuss the following forms :—*are; wert; could; methinks; durst; ought; distraught.* (1867).

1067. Discuss the forms :—*brethren; seamstress; indices; fisherman; cherry; kine; swine; cherubim; riches; uttermost.* (1885).

1068. Derive *next, last, best, further, rather.* (1883).

1069. Tell what you know of the origin of each of the following words, with comment upon any fact in the history of English that it might serve to illustrate:—*Avon, Chester, Grimsby, cloister, minster, cherry, beef, nuisance, cousin, potion, poison.* (1884).

1070. Use the words *book, but, thou, he, who, why, enough, feet, ought, knew, best,* as examples of some means of distinguishing words in modern English that belonged to the language in its earliest Teutonic form. (1882).

1071. Derive the words:—*lady*; *madam*; *sir*; *husband*; *woman*; *bachelor*; *lass*; *cousin*; *uncle*; *archbishop.* (1884).

1072. What is the etymology of the following words:—*under, over, every, eleven, twenty, least, near?* (1885).

1073. Discuss the etymology of *bridegroom, children, could, eleven, goose, hers, mice, once, songstress, vixen.* (1888).

1074. Show the different usages of the following words, and account for these by derivation:—*alight, burden, broil, wind, blow, race.* (1889).

1075. Give the original and derivative meaning of the following words:—*cynical, puny, trivial, agony, pagan, villain, heathen, economy, tally.* (1889).

1076. Give the derivation of the following words:—*alive, dead, many, alert, entail, result, heresy, knife, ideal, key, bury, rather, king, lady.* (1888).

1077. Give the origin of the following words, and show how they have come to bear their present meaning:—*prose, poetry, epic, lyric, dramatic.* (1889.)

1078. Derive *Well-a-day, Alas.* (1882).

1079. Give the etymology of the following pronouns, and show how their use has varied:—*This, that, what, which, whose.* (1885).

1080. Give the derivations of *add, condition, deodand, editor, recondite, surrender.* (1860).

H 2

1081. Point out the letter-changes which have taken place in the following words :—*gossip*; *number*; *tyrant*; *fee*. (1882).

1082. Give a dozen examples of English words spelt so as to indicate the etymology rather than the sound. Criticise or defend such a mode of spelling. (1865).

1083. Which letters in the following words are unpronounced ? Whence do they come ? and why are they retained in spelling ?—*debt, handsome, chronicle, neighbour, hymn, receipt, psalm, viscount.* (1862).

1084. It is said that to introduce a system of purely phonetic spelling into English would be to obliterate traces of the history of many words. Discuss the present orthography of the following words, and show how far this assertion is true concerning them :—*chronometer, phantom, city, honour, syntax, bough, debt, who, vitiate, rheumatism.* (1873).

XII. Prosody.

1085. What is Prosody? When are words said to rhyme? Distinguish between true and false rhymes. (1875, 1883).

1086. Explain the use of accent in English verse. What is rhyme? Distinguish between perfect and imperfect rhymes. Describe the measure that is known commonly in England as Blank Verse. (1883).

1087. Distinguish between Syntax and Prosody. Define a perfect Rhyme. (1880).

1088. Discuss and illustrate the conditions of perfect Rhyme. (1873).

1089. Define "metre," and state how your definition applies to "Piers Ploughman," to "Paradise Lost," to "Homer's Iliad." (1859).

1090. Distinguish between Rhyme, Alliteration, and Metre; and show how each has affected poetical expression in England. (1888).

1091. Write a few notes on the chief English Metres. (1881).

1092. Distinguish between Accent and Emphasis. What is meant by Rhyme, Double rhyme, Quantity, Alliteration? Give an instance of the Pause in Blank Verse. (1882).

1093. Accent in English (a) modifies the meaning of words, (b) forms compounds, (c) sometimes fixes the date of the introduction of words, and (d) regulates our metre. Illustrate this statement. (1860).

1094. Scan the lines :—

> " And out again I curve and flow
>   To join the brimming river,
> For men may come, and men may go,
>   But I go on for ever."

Do you regard this verse as a perfect example of the metre in which it is written ? Give reasons for your answers. (1860).

1095. Describe the metre of the following stanza :—

> " We look before and after,
>   And pine for what is not ;
> Our sincerest laughter
>   With some pain is fraught ;
> Our sweetest songs are those that tell of saddest thought."

(1883).

APPENDICES.

A.

ADVICE TO INTENDING CANDIDATES AS TO THE BEST
MODE OF PREPARING FOR THE EXAMINATION.

IT will be seen from the preceding Questions
that the "General History and Grammatical Structure of the English Language," as the subject is
defined in the Regulations of the University of
London, is a term open to considerable latitude of
interpretation. The Examiners, too, who are elected
periodically, do not all interpret the definition in
the same way or look at the subject from the same
point of view. This is, on the whole, satisfactory,
for it tends to encourage real teaching as opposed to
cramming. At the same time it must be acknow-
ledged that to answer completely and thoroughly
the whole of a paper, or the required portions, when
a choice of questions is allowed (as is the case in
this particular subject, and should be in every
branch of the Examination), would usually occupy
more time than is given. This is a point to be
borne in mind.

The Matriculation questions are reducible to six
classes :—

I. Dictation.
II. History of the Language.
III. Etymology, Phonology, and Permutation
of Sounds.
IV. The Parts of Speech.
V. Syntax.
VI. Analysis.

Questions are also sometimes set on Derivation and Prosody.

Dictation, which was formerly a *sine qua non*,
seems to have fallen into disfavour for the present,
judging from the last two Examinations; but it is
hardly necessary to warn Candidates that correct
spelling is of the utmost importance and should be
carefully attended to. Perhaps one of the best
methods of mastering the difficulties of spelling is
for the Candidate to read over, three or four times,
very carefully, a page of some good author, writing
down and afterwards rigorously testing himself in
the spelling of all words with which he is not
thoroughly acquainted, or which present any difficulty arising from peculiarity of either spelling
or pronunciation. Short books, or parts of books,
read in this way will be of great assistance, should
he have to depend on himself for instruction.

There are so many books on the English Language that it becomes a somewhat difficult task to
select those that are most suitable to students preparing for this examination. One should always try
to get up at least a little more of a subject than is
likely to be asked for. The following books will be
found to be of great assistance, but it must be re-
membered that no single work will be sufficient by
itself :—

MORRIS'S ELEMENTARY LESSONS ON HISTORICAL

APPENDICES. 105

ENGLISH GRAMMAR. To be used as a text-book, with additions, for aspirants to honours, from other sources.

MASON's *English Grammar.* The most advanced of the four published by that author.

FLEMING's *Analysis of the English Language.* Useful for advanced students.

DANIEL's *Grammar, History and Derivation of the English Language.* Good and very full of useful matter.

MEIKLEJOHN's *Book of the English Language.* Good and suggestive, with the great merit of brevity.

HEWITT's *Manual of our Mother-Tongue.* Useful as a special book for students who want a manual for Matriculation.

ANGUS's *Handbook of the English Tongue.* A little out of date, but containing suggestive matter.

HODGSON's *Errors in the use of English.* A good Syntax guide.

DALGLEISH's *Grammatical Analysis.* A cheap and short manual.

ALFORD's *The Queen's English.* An almost unique work in fixing the classical usage of English words and expressions.

Having obtained such of the above as appear most desirable, or are within reach, the Candidate should have his note-book always at hand, in which to enter condensed extracts, not merely from the text-book but also other books, bearing on the particular part of the subject under notice. Making notes is far and away better than simply scoring books; the memory invariably retains a greater hold of what is written. But note-making, like anything else in which it is desired to achieve success, to be useful must be methodical. Spasmodic notes on separate pieces of paper are simply productive of vexation of spirit—they are never to be found when wanted. Text-books should not be made to serve the extra purpose of note-books, nor should the notes be too lengthy or too abundant, but judiciously selected. One side only of the note-book should be used; the other will then be at disposal for any additional notes that may need to be added. It is sometimes advisable to state the sources from which information has been obtained, especially as there are several points in the study of English, on which authorities differ.

Using, then, Morris's *Elementary Lessons* as the text-book, as we have suggested, and having several times read over a chapter or so at a time, let the Candidate test his knowledge by *writing* the answers to some of the questions contained in this book, that bear on that special portion. Writing the answers cannot be too much insisted on; mentally answering the questions is all but useless. In order to be successful in the Examination itself, the Candidate must accustom himself to do exactly the sort of work that will be required of him; to *assume* that he can answer any question is a mistake. Difficulties frequently do not appear until he begins to write his answer, and are then apt to throw him into a state of nervousness and perplexity. The art of intelligibly expressing knowledge on paper must be acquired. The want of this is a very frequent cause of failure. It is easy to put on paper a certain amount of more or less accurate information in a slipshod manner, without arrangement or plan : it is the result of training to compress, arrange, and systematize this same matter.

And it cannot be too forcibly impressed on all aspirants to honours that they must not only know their work, but be able to state their information · clearly.

We have already spoken of Dictation. Of the other classes into which the subject is divided above, the History of the language is one of the most important. In this, as well as in all matters bearing on Philology, it is well to avoid all antiquated ideas and theories, even if they are not very old, as reckoned by years. Philology has made great strides in recent times. Grimm's Law will demand special attention, and too much stress cannot be laid on the necessity of thoroughly mastering the *principles* of Syntax and Analysis. A knowledge of principles is far better than the mere learning of rules—committing so many formulæ to memory without understanding what they mean or the reason why. In the matter of Derivation *Morris* and *Daniel* will be found very useful. Questions are given sometimes, but very rarely, on Prosody. And, since it is the usual practice to give fifteen or sixteen questions, ten only of which are to be answered, the candidate should select those that best show his knowledge.

B.

HINTS TO A CANDIDATE AS TO DEALING WITH THE PAPER.

In all examinations time is a most important element: it must, therefore, be economised. Look somewhat rapidly, but by no means carelessly, through the paper; then mark the requisite number, consisting of such as best represent the various subdivisions of the subject, and the answers to which will prove to the examiners that you possess the requisite knowledge. You will soon find a question that you feel you can answer at once. Write your answer, and this will give you confidence to attack the rest of the paper. Always leave a line or two between the answers, as you may wish to insert something afterwards. Pick out another question, and so continue, and you will most probably find that at the expiration of, say, half the allotted time, you will have answered considerably more than half the requisite portion of the paper. You will now probably find that three or four questions remain, the answers to which will demand the exercise of more thought. Take in succession those that present the fewest difficulties, and you will eventually find that you have answered the whole paper with comparative ease.

See that you understand the questions, and what the examiners wish to get from you. Remember that it is *answers to their questions* that they want. The answers should, therefore, be to the point and concise, all irrelevant matter, tautology, and mere verbiage being rigorously excluded. It is quality, not quantity, that pays. Never forget, before leaving your seat, to read over very carefully all your answers. In the hurry of writing, errors may have been made which you can easily correct, or new ideas may occur to you which may enable you to supplement some of your answers.

How *not to do a paper* is either to endeavour to answer the questions in the order in which they are printed, or to pick out what appears to you to be a difficult question, and one that you think will score heavily if successfully answered, and work away at that first. In this way much valuable time will be spent, your mind worried and unfitted to grapple with the rest of the paper, and perhaps after a long struggle you may find yourself unable to answer the question. Disheartened by want of success, you see the whole paper before you and nothing done. You try to make up for lost time, make a rush at another question, perhaps with no better success, by which time you will, most likely, be thoroughly "muddled."

C.

AN IDEAL EXAMINATION PAPER.

ACTING on the subdivisions of the subject laid down in Appendix A, such questions as the following (not taken from an examination paper) will be found to be fairly representative :—

1. Write and punctuate the following passage read by the Examiner.

" He publicly protested that he was no mover in the matter that the first steps had been taken without his privvity ; that he could not advise the Parliament to strike the blow but that he submitted his own feelings to the force of circumstances which seemed to him to indicate the purposes of Providence : it has been the fashion to consider these professions as instances of the hippocricy which is vulgarly impeuted to him. But even those who pronounce him a hippocrit will scarcely venture to call him a fool, they are therefore bound to show that he had some purpose to serve by secretly stifhmulating the army to take that coarse which he did not venture openly to recommend. It would be absurd to suppose that he who was never by his respectable enemies, represented as wantonly cruel or implackably Vindictive, would have taken the most important step of his Life under the influence of mere malevolents."—MACAULAY, "History of England," ch. i.

[*The above passage is printed as it might, and ought not to, be written and punctuated.*]

2. Estimate the place of English among allied languages.

3. Give a pedigree of the English language, which shall show from what sources, and at what epochs, it has been successively enriched.

4. Define the terms *letter, vowel, diphthong, word, phrase, clause, sentence.*

5. Classify Consonants, and define the terms you use.

6. State the principles on which Grimm's Law is founded. Formulate the Law, and illustrate it in Guttural letters.

7. Classify Adverbs.

8. Comment on six cases of irregularity in the comparison of Adjectives.

9. Compare English in respect of the formation of Gender with any other language with which you are acquainted.

10. Tell what you know of the history of *Self.* What part of speech is it ?   Explain its construction.

11. Discuss the use of *shall* and *will* as signs of the Future Tense.

12. Correct or justify the following, giving your reason in each case :—

(Ten phrases or sentences.)

13. Analyse the following :—

(Two sentences ; one fairly easy, the other complicated.)

14. Discuss the forms :—*Brethren, Seamstress, Indices, Its, Kine, Swine, Riches, Uttermost.*

D.

AN ACTUAL EXAMINATION PAPER.

The following is the paper set at the Examination, held in June, 1887 :—

Examiners, { HENRY CRAIK, Esq., C.B., LL.D.
Prof. JOHN W. HALES, M.A.

[N.B.—*Questions* 1, 10, 13 *and* 15, *must be attempted by every one, and of the rest not more than* Six.]

1. Write out and punctuate the passage read by the Examiner.
2. Explain and illustrate the terms Synthetic and Analytic as applied to Languages. By which would you describe the English language as it now is ?
3. Distinguish between the Teutonic and the Romance elements of the English Vocabulary ; and write two short sentences, one containing no words of Romance origin, the other none of Teutonic. Which is the easier sentence to write, and why ?
4. Point out some of the inconsistencies of English Spelling, and of English Pronunciation. How have such inconsistencies arisen ?
5. Classify the Consonantal letters. What is meant by Grimn's Law, and to which group does it apply ? How would you class the letter H ?
6. Give instances of Common Nouns becoming Proper, and of Proper becoming Common. How does the Possessive Case differ from the Genitive ?
7. In what two ways may Adjectives be compared ? How do there come to be two ways ? By what terms would you denote them? State the general rule as to their use.

8. Discuss the ordinary definition of a Pronoun. What other definition has been suggested? Distinguish between the forms *my* and *mine*. Which is the older form? What similar pairs are there?

9. Explain the terms:—Voice, Mood, Infinitive. Show how frequently in English Transitive verbs are used Intransitively, and *vice versa*. Mention some Causative verbs.

10. Distinguish between the Strong and the Weak Conjugations. By what other names are they known? Which is the older? Which is the living one? To which do these verbs belong: fight, think, bare, bear, catch, teach, reach, beseech, hang, fly?

11. Parse *must* in " He says he *must* go," and " He said he *must* go; " and mention some other verbs that are similarly unchanged. What do you know of the verbs *quoth, wot, thinks* in methinks?|

12. Discuss the phrases : He found them *fled*, horses *and all*—Fight *away* my men—*Get you gone* —I give you this *to boot*—*To oversleep oneself*—How did he *come by* such a fortune?

13. Criticise and correct the following pieces of Grammar and Style :—

> (*a.*) Books that we can at a glance carry off all that is in them, are worse than useless for discipline.
>
> (*b.*) He preferred to know the worst than to dream the best.
>
> (*c.*) Humanity seldom or ever shows itself in inferior dispositions.
>
> (*d.*) You have already been informed of the sale of Ford's theatre, where Mr. Lincoln was assassinated, for religious purposes.
>
> (*e.*) The Moor seizing a bolster, full of rage and jealousy, smothered her.

(*f.*) Nor do I know any one with whom I can converse more pleasantly, or I would prefer as my companion.

14. In what various ways may the Subject of a sentence be enlarged? In what the Predicate extended? Compose a sentence to illustrate your answers.

15. Analyse:—

(*a.*) The Sea that bares her bosom to the Moon,
The winds that will be howling at all hours,
And are upgather'd now like sleeping flowers,
For this, for everything, we are out of tune.

(*b.*) In the olden days, in which distance could not be vanquished without toil but in which the toil was rewarded, there were few moments of which the recollection was more fondly cherished by the traveller than that which brought him within sight of Venice. Not but that the aspect of the city itself was generally the source of some slight disappointment.

E.

It may be useful here to append some classifications which are repeatedly asked for in the Matriculation Examinations of the University of London, recommending the candidate to remember that they may or may not form part of his selected questions, according as he does or does not find them easy to recollect. Accuracy here is of vital importance.

I

TABLE OF THE ARYAN LANGUAGES.

Asiatic.

I. HINDU
- Sanscrit (dead).
- Hindi, Hindustani, Bengali, Mahratti.
- Cingalese.
- Gypsy Dialect.

II. IRANIAN
- Zend.
- Persian.

III. KELTIC
- Armorican.
- Welsh.
- Erse.
- Gaelic.
- Manx.

European.

CLASSICAL

IV. ITALIC
- Latin.
- RomanceDialects sprung from Latin:—
  - Italian.
  - French.
  - Spanish and Portuguese.
  - Roumansch.
  - Wallachian.

V. HELLENIC
- Ancient Greek.
- Modern Greek.

VI. TEUTONIC
- Low German—English, Dutch, Flemish.
- Scandinavian—Icelandic, Swedish, Danish, Norwegian.
- High-German—Modern German.

VII. LETTIC
- Old Prussian (dead).
- Lettish.

VIII. SLAVONIC
- Russian.
- Polish.
- Bohemian.

The stock underlined twice is our own. The stocks once underlined are those with which we are incidentally connected.

F.

THE PARTS OF SPEECH.

1.—NOUNS.

(*a.*) ACCORDING TO FORM :—

    Primitive. Derived. Compound.

(*b.*) ACCORDING TO MEANING :—

PROPER. { Strictly [*Milton*].
{ Becoming common ["*some mute inglorious Milton.*"]

COMMON. ⎧ Class names { sensible [*knife*].'
                            { rational [*conqueror*].
       ⎨ Collective { singular [*mob*].
                    { noun of Multitude [*clergy*].
       ⎪ Materials [*iron*].
       ⎪ Quantity [*yard*].
       ⎩ Agents [*dreamer*].

ABSTRACT. ⎧ States [*death*].
        ⎨ Acts [*talking*].
        ⎪ Qualities [*goodness*].
        ⎩ Degree [*excess*].

———

2.—ADJECTIVES.

ACCORDING
TO STRUCTURE OR
FORM.
- Simple [black].
- Derived [beauteous].
- Compound [sea-green].

ACCORDING TO
FORMATION AND
MEANING.
- Common [good].
- Proper [English].
- Numeral [three].
- Pronominal [each].
- Participial [enticing].
- Compound [web-footed].

ACCORDING TO
MEANING.

Definitive
- General [a].
- Particular [the].

Qualitative
- Privative [homeless].
- Diminutive [childish].
- Augmentative [hopeful].
- Positive [learned].
- Causative [terrific].
- Potential [pleasurable].

Quantitative
- Definite
  - Cardinal [two].
  - Ordinal [first].
  - Multiplicative [double].
- Indefinite [few].
- Distributive [each, every].

3.—PRONOUNS.

ACCORDING TO FORM.
- Simple [I, me].
- Derived [my].
- Compound [myself].

ACCORDING TO
MEANING.

Adjective
- Demonstrative [this].
- Relative [who].
- Interrogative [who?].
- Possessive [my].
- Reflexive [self].
- Distributive [each].
- Reciprocal [each other].
- Indefinite [any].

Substantive
- Personal [I].
- Reflexive [self].
- Indefinite [aught].

4.—THE VERB.

Impersonal.
- Impersonal [*methinks*].
- Unipersonal [*it rains*].

Personal.

ACCORDING TO QUALITY.
- Substantive [*be*] (asserts what things are).
- Adjective [*glitter*] (asserts a quality).

ACCORDING TO RELATION.
- Transitive [*warn*].
- Intransitive [*walk*].
- Auxiliary [*can*].

ACCORDING TO FORM.
- Regular or Weak [*love*].
- Irregular or Strong [*bear*].
- Redundant [*clothe*].
- Defective [*may*].

ACCORDING TO MEANING.
- Active, Passive, Middle [*it tastes*].
- Neuter [*sleep*].
- Reflexive [*behave yourself*].
- Causative [*fell*].
- Intensive [*bluster*].
- Diminutive [*glimmer*].
- Inceptive [*effervesce*].
- Frequentative [*agitate*].

ACCORDING TO ORIGIN.
- Primitive.
- Derived.

5.—ADVERBS.

ACCORDING TO ORIGIN.
- Primitive
- Derived [*otherwise*].
- Compound [*wherever*].

ACCORDING TO MEANING.
- Time [*once, always, meanwhile*].
- Place [*here, hither, hence, firstly*].
- Quantity or Degree [*too, exactly*].
- Quality [*well, therefore, perhaps*].

SHOWING CONNECTION.
- Conjunctional.
- Simply Attributive.

6.—PREPOSITIONS.

ACCORDING TO STRUCTURE.
{ Simple [*in*].
Compound [*about*].
Verbal [*notwithstanding*]. }

ACCORDING TO MEANING.
{ *Express relations of*
Position [*on, to, over*].
Time [*till*].
Cause, Instrumentality, Agency [*by, through*].
Degree [*throughout*].
Direction [*towards*]. }

7.—CONJUNCTIONS.

ACCORDING TO STRUCTURE.
{ Simple [*if*].
Derived [*either*].
Compound [*how-be-it*]. }

ACCORDING TO MEANING.
{
Co-ordinate. {
Copulative [*and*].
Negative [*neither*].
Alternative [*either*].
Adversative [*still*].
Illative [*therefore*]. }

Subordinate. {
Time [*when, whilst*].
Place [*thence*].
Manner or Degree [*how, than*].
Cause [*in order that, because*]. }
}

G.

THE FORMS IN -ING.

The following table shows how the confusion arose
between the Simple and Gerundial Infinitives, the
Active Participle, and the Verbal Noun :—

A.D.	Simple Infinitive.	Gerundial Infinitive.	Active Participle.	Verbal Noun.
1100	-an	to -anne	-ende, -inde	-ung
1250	-en, -c	to { -enne / -ene / -en / -e	-inde	-yng
1350	to -e	to { -ene / -e	-inge	-yng, -ing
1500	to *as the sole sign of the Infinitive*		-inge	-ing
1600	to [hear] = [hear]ing			

THE END.

II. K. Lewis, Printer, 136, Gower Street, London, W.C.

PRINTED BY
H. K. LEWIS, 136 GOWER STREET
LONDON, W.C.

PREFACE.

In this edition the Questions have been brought down to the present year, but space has been gained by combining similar ones, the dates being retained. When more than one date occurs, it does not of course follow that the same words have been used on each occasion. As the publication has been somewhat delayed, I have added in an Appendix the questions set at the Examination which has just been held.

In some instances I have indicated the sources, not necessarily the only ones, but probably the best, from which answers to the questions on English History may be obtained.

F. W. L.

July, 1886.

QUESTIONS

ON

HISTORY AND GEOGRAPHY.

A.—ENGLISH HISTORY.

I. Principal Events.

1. Give a short account of the Ancient Britons. To what sources are we mainly indebted for the knowledge which we possess of this portion of history? Mention the period which is embraced by each of the works to which you refer. (1846).

2. Give a brief account of the inhabitants of this Island before and when the Romans arrived. (1884).

3. What was the condition of the Britons, as described by Caesar when he visited this Island? (1876, '77).

4. What were Caesar's inducements for landing in Britain? What account did he give of the Island? What improvements did the Romans effect in it? (1878).

5. Mention the most important events in the history of Britain under the Romans, connected with the names of the Emperor Claudius, Agricola, Septimius Severus, and Carausius. (1857).

6. Name the tribes found in Britain by the first Roman invaders, and specify the modern Counties which answer to the seat of each tribe. (1872).

B

7. "After a war of about forty years, the far greater part of the Island submitted to the Roman yoke. Neither the fortitude of Caractacus, nor the despair of Boadicea, nor the fanaticism of the Druids, could resist the steady progress of the Imperial Generals." Explain the historical allusions contained in this passage. By which of the Roman Emperors was Britain visited? (1848).

8. What events in Britain are associated with the names of Cassivelaunus, Caractacus, Boadicea? (1884).

9. What is the earliest historical notice which we have of the persecution of British Christians on account of their religious opinions? (1847).

10. How much of England was occupied by the Romans; and in what circumstances did it cease to be so occupied? (1854, '58, '73).

11. Give a short account of Britain from the first authentic notices of it till the period of its final abandonment by the Romans. (1844).

12. What efforts were made by the inhabitants of this Island, at different times, to throw off the Roman yoke? (1876).

13. What had been done by the Romans towards the civilisation of this country before it fell under the hands of the Teutonic invaders? (1874).

14. Mention the successive efforts made by the Britons to resist the Roman and Saxon invaders. (1877).

15. What remains have we—roads, settlements, buildings, literature—of the Roman occupation of Britain? (1860, '80, '84, '85).

16. To what sources must we go for the history of the Roman occupation of Britain? What traces has it left behind, not only in material remains, but also in political institutions? (1880).

17. What information respecting the early history

of our country have we obtained from Latin writers? (1863).

18. Sketch the history of this Island before its conquest by low German tribes. (1885).

19. At what period did the Angles and Saxons settle in this country? What religion did they bring with them? When were they converted to Christianity? By whose agency, and by what means? And what were the social and political effects of their conversion? (1877).

20. Give the generally received account of the manner in which the Heptarchy was formed. What objection has been made to the term? Give from Athenian history a parallel instance of the consolidation of a number of petty states. (1856).

21. Give some account of the introduction of Christianity into this Island through the efforts of Gregory the Great. (1878).

22. Enumerate the earliest kings of the following kingdoms:—Kent, Northumbria, Wessex, and Mercia. (1876).

23. Explain how the kingdoms of Kent, Northumbria, Wessex, and Mercia were consolidated into one—by what king, and at what time. (1876).

24. What causes led to the supremacy of Wessex? When was that supremacy established? by whom? and with what results? (1876).

25. Account for the uncivilised state of England when Alfred ascended the throne. (1880).

26. What benefits did Alfred the Great procure for his country? On what grounds has this distinction of "the Great" been assigned to him? (1878).

27. Describe the work of Alfred (1) in resisting the Danish invaders, (2) in internal administration. (1886).

28. What was the extent of Alfred's dominions at the time of his death? Who were the most dis-

tinguished of his Anglo-Saxon successors? (1848). [*Tait*].

29. Give a sketch of the state of Britain from the period of its abandonment by the Romans till that of the death of Alfred the Great. Describe the limits of each of the petty kingdoms composing the Saxon Heptarchy. (1845).

30. Give a summary of the chief events in the history of this Island from the accession of Egbert to the death of Alfred the Great. (1874).

31. Give some account of the reign of Edgar. (1882).

32. What illustrations can you give of the connection between England and the Continent before the year 900? (1885). [*Powell*].

33. Give an account of the reign of Edward the Confessor. (1858).

34. Describe the state of this country at the death of Edward the Confessor, and the preparations made for its invasion by William the Norman. (1878).

35. Give a sketch of the history of Great Britain from the withdrawal of the Romans to the landing of William the Conqueror, having regard especially to the Geographical distribution of the races which occupied the British Isles during that period. (1879).

36. Give a brief sketch of the Anglo-Saxon history from the time of Alfred to the Norman Conquest. (1857).

37. From what original sources do we derive our acquaintance with the state of England during the Anglo-Saxon period? Mention the general character of each of the works to which you refer, the age in which it was written, and the portion of time which it embraces. (1851).

38. Derive the name England; and explain as well as you can how that name came to prevail. (1884, '85).

39. What do you know concerning the relations between England and Normandy before the Norman Conquest? (1881).

40. What had been William I.'s pretext for invading Britain? Was England treated by him as a conquered country? Give proofs of your assertion. (1844, '45, '49).

41. What were the difficulties William I. had to encounter before the conquest of England was completed? (1879).

42. To what causes, besides the prowess of the Normans, is the dissolution of the Anglo-Saxon rule to be attributed? (1878).

43. Describe briefly the changes introduced by William I. (1876).

44. What steps were taken by William I. to consolidate his conquest? (1874).

45. What were the occasion and the object of the compiling of *Domesday Book*? Does it prove anything as to the results of the conquest? (1881).

46. When did William the Conqueror die? and where was he buried? (1867).

47. Give the names of the first three Norman kings, with the dates of their accession; and show what circumstances in the reign of each tended to modify the severity of the Norman Conquest. (1875).

48. Enumerate, with dates, the kings of the Anglo-Norman period. Give a brief sketch of the character of the third in that line. (1856).

49. Give a list of the Plantagenet kings, and describe very briefly the character of each. (1854, '68).

50. State the grounds of the contest between Henry II. and Becket. Describe the circumstances and consequences of the death of that prelate. (1848, '84).

✓ 51. State the principal events of the reign of Henry II. (1857, '66, '71).

52. What were the Crusades? To what extent did they influence English history, socially or commercially? (1862). [*Ross*].

53. Give the dates of the first and last Crusade. (1868).

54. Give a short account of the Crusades, and of the part played in them by Englishmen. (1872, '84).

55. " The talents and even the virtues of her six first French kings were a curse to England. The follies and vices of the seventh were her salvation." Show the truth of this observation, and point out the salutary effects produced upon England by her separation from Normandy. (1856).

56. Give some account of the reign of King John. (1873).

57. When was the Pontifical authority at its greatest height in England; and in what act was it most conspicuously exerted? (1849).

58. Narrate the conflict between the Pope and King John up to the surrender of the crown by the latter. Explain clearly the meaning of that act. (1882).

59. Relate the most remarkable events which took place in the reign of Henry II., and also in that of Edward I. (1852).

60. Give the dates of the Roman, Anglo-Saxon, Norman, and English, periods of our History: add your reason for the date you give as the beginning of the last. (1859).

61. Fix the date of the commencement of the English nation, as a complete nation. Adduce reasons in favor of the date you adopt. (1854).

62. " The History of the English nation commences in the 13th century." Explain this remark,

and give in the form of a chronological table a list of the principal events of that century. (1863).

63. Write a short account of the chief historical events in the reign of King John. (1881).

64. What was the origin, and what were the consequences, of the disputes between John and the English barons ? (1855).

65. Give an account of the chief political and military events which distinguish the reign of Edward I. (1873).

66. What were the claims of Edward III. to the Crown of France ? How did he attempt to establish them, and with what results ? (1876).

67. Give the date of the treaty of Bretigni. Explain the events which led to it, and give some account of its provisions. (1877, '81, '82).

68. Give, with dates, a summary of the principal events in the reign of Edward III. ; and mention the names of the most famous men of his time. (1864, '69).

69. At the close of the reign of Edward III. what was the extent of the English Dominions here and on the continent ? (1874).

70. What were the announced objects of Wat Tyler's insurrection ? . (1884).

71. Mention the principal events which occurred between the time when Richard II. became absolute, and his renunciation of the Crown. (1856).

72. Give an account of the Popular Insurrections under Richard II., and compare them with those under Henry VI. (1876).

73. In whose reign did Wickliffe attempt to effect a Reformation of the Church in this country ? When did that Reformation take place ? (1864).

74. Tell the chief causes of the deposition of Richard II. (1870, '81).

75. Describe and contrast the opposition offered

to Edward II. and Richard II. respectively. (1886).

76. What were the points in dispute between the Yorkists and Lancastrians? How did these terms originate? (1874).

77. Tell what you know of the political relations between England and Scotland in the reign of Henry IV. (1884). [*Ross*].

78. By what means did this country lose its possessions in France in the 15th century? (1874).

79. Give the particulars of Jack Cade's Insurrection, and compare it with that of Wat Tyler. (1879).

80. What do you know concerning the history of religion in the Lancastrian reigns? (1881). [*Gairdner*].

81. What was the origin of the House of Tudor? Whence was the name derived? What changes took place in the religious and political condition of the nation during their rule? (1878).

82. What were the political troubles to which Henry VII. was exposed during his reign? What was the character of this king? (1877).

83. Describe the state of Ireland in the time of Henry VII., the mode of administering its government, and the circumstances under which the English power was subsequently established in that island. (1861). [*Collier*].

84. Give the date of the accession of Henry VIII. Mention the names of his wives, children, and chief ministers; adding the fate of each. (1868, '80).

85. Name the successive wives of Henry VIII., and describe as nearly as you can from the king's point of view the manner of his severance from each of them. (1883).

86. What was the state of public opinion as to re-

ligion at the beginning of the reign of Henry VIII.? Give a short account of (1) his controversy with Luther, (2) his divorce from Catherine, and (3) his separation from the Church of Rome. (1847).

87. Tell briefly the history of the divorce of Henry VIII. from Catherine of Arragon, and point out some of its consequences. (1872).

88. On what occasion did one of our sovereigns receive the title of Defender of the faith? (1870).

89. Give some account of the steps which led to the suppression of the Monasteries; of the Statesman who first conceived, and of the Statesman who executed, the work. (1880, '83).

90. Give some account of the confiscation of Monastic or other Ecclesiastical Estates at the time of the Reformation; and describe the purposes to which they were applied. (1872).

91. What kings, before the Reformation, especially favoured or resisted the Papal authority in England, and by what measures? (1879). [Guest].

92. Discuss the causes of the great movement known as the Reformation. (1884).

93. What steps were taken by Henry VIII. towards establishing the Reformation in England? (1875, '82).

94. What was the "Pilgrimage of Grace"? How did Aske become the leader in this insurrection? Describe his interview with the king, and his subsequent fate. (1858).

95. What were the most remarkable events in the reign of Henry VIII., subsequently to the fall of Wolsey? What were the chief political consequences of the dissolution, and alienation of the endowments, of the Monasteries? (1848).

96. Exactly how far had the Reformation proceeded at the death of Henry VIII.? How far was

Queen Mary able to undo what had by her time been done? (1883).

97. What do you know of the history of the Reformation in Scotland, up to the time of Queen Mary's arrival there? (1882).

98. What were the political relations between England and Scotland during the reigns of Henry VII. and Henry VIII. ? (1872).

99. What events led to the Execution of Mary, Queen of Scots ? (1872).

100. Enumerate the causes of the quarrel between England and Spain in the sixteenth century. (1883, '85).

101. Narrate the chief events in English History which arose out of the relations between England and Spain during the reign of Elizabeth. (1871, '73).

102. Write a brief history of this country from 1580 to 1590. (1884). [Tait].

103. Recount the events of the year 1587. (1858).

104. Explain the relations between England and Spain that led to the equipment of the Spanish Armada. (1883). [Creighton].

105. Indicate briefly the foreign policy of Queen Elizabeth. (1880). [Tait].

106. What assistance was given by Elizabeth to Protestants abroad ? (1881). [Hume].

107. Mention some of the more important events in the reign of Elizabeth, with the real or approximate dates. (1848, '74).

108. Give some account of affairs in Ireland during the reign of Elizabeth, with particular reference to the expedition of the Earl of Essex. (1884). [Green].

109. What were the most remarkable events which occurred in England from the year 1527 to the end of the reign of Elizabeth ? (1850).

110. Describe the progress of the Reformation during the reign of Elizabeth. (1847).

111. How long did the Tudor dynasty last? State in their order the most memorable events during this period. (1875).

112. Describe the conduct of the Tudor princes towards the nobles and the church. (1877).

113. In what year, and under what circumstances respectively, did Scotland and Ireland become parts of the same empire with England? (1849).

114. Explain the occasion and the manner of what is called the " Plantation of Ulster." (1881). [*Hume*].

115. Give reasons why the importance of England ought to have increased after the accession of James I. How do you account for its diminution? (1856). [*Tait*].

116. What were the principal charges made against Bacon? and how far were they substantiated? (1861). [*Hume*].

117. What plots were set on foot against James I. in this country? Who were mainly concerned in them? (1867, '78).

118. By what ministers was James I. successively governed? (1878).

119. What do you know concerning the foreign policy of James I.? (1882). [*Tait*].

120. Give a summary of the chief events, and describe the most prominent public men and measures, of the reign of James I. (1871).

121. What were the successive subjects of contention between Charles I. and his Parliaments? How were they eventually determined? (1855, '78, '83). [*Tait*].

122. Explain what is meant by Ship-money. When, and how, did it originate? On what grounds

was it levied by Charles I.; and on what grounds was it resisted? (1875).

123. Describe, with dates, the chief events in the history of the Parliamentary struggle between the Petition of Right, in 1629, and the outbreak of the Civil War. (1885).

124. Tell briefly the history of the period of twelve years between the third and fourth Parliaments of Charles I. (1883).

125. What were the causes which led to the trials of John Hampden and the Earl of Strafford respectively? (1866, '72).

126. When did the Long Parliament commence? What circumstances led to its establishment? What were the motives which induced the King to consent to its demands in the first instance? Mention some of the chief measures enacted by it, and the time and circumstances of its extinction. (1877).

127. When was the Long Parliament opened? When and how was it closed? Set down, with their dates, but without details, any five events that form part of its history. (1884).

128. What were the principal parties of which the Long Parliament, under Charles I., was composed? Mention the names of the leading men of each party. Describe its most remarkable proceedings previously to the breaking out of the Civil War. (1849).

129. Point out the principal phases of the struggle between Charles I. and the Parliament, both before and after the commencement of the Civil War. (1851).

130. Into what parties was the nation divided in the reign of Charles I., and what were the religious and political principles of each? (1875).

131. State the leading events of the Civil War between Charles I. and the Parliament; also the causes, circumstances and consequences of the death of the King. (1844).

132. Describe as fully as you can the characteristic ideas of the two contending parties in the Civil War of the seventeenth century. What were the immediate, what the final, results? (1884).

133. In the contention of Charles I. with his Parliament, among what classes and in what counties did the strength of the contending parties respectively lie? Give the dates of the more important battles, and show in what counties they were fought. (1875). [*Ross*].

134. Of what parties in the nation were Essex, Fairfax, and Cromwell the respective leaders? On what grounds did these parties oppose the King? (1876, '80).

135. What soldiers, or other men of eminence, took the sides of Charles and of Cromwell respectively, in the Civil Wars? Name the occasions on which they severally distinguished themselves. (1874).

136. Mention the parties, civil and religious, into which this nation was divided during the Civil Wars, and their more eminent leaders; showing in what points they differed from each other. (1879).

137. Who were the "Five Members"? What were the consequences which flowed from their arrest? (1865, '82).

138. What was the purport of the Solemn League and Covenant? and what its effects upon England? (1876, '78).

139. What causes drove the Scotch into rebellion in the reign of Charles I. ? (1876).

140. Describe the circumstances which induced Charles I. to consent to the demands of the Long Parliament. (1877).

141. What reasons were alleged for the trial and execution of Charles I. ? What steps were taken by his enemies to overawe the Parliament and the people? (1876).

142. Give an account of the political trials in England in the reign of Charles I.   (1857).

143. Mention the chief particulars relating to the trial and death of Charles I.   What circumstances mainly contributed to the Restoration of that monarch's family ?   (1848).

144. Give an account of the principal events in Irish history from the year 1640 to the year 1650.   (1881).   [*Collier*].

145. State the causes, and narrate the progress of the Irish Insurrection in the reign of Charles I.   (1882).

146. Account for the discontent in Ireland in the reign of Charles I., and in Scotland in the reigns of Charles I. and Charles II.   (1880).   [*Ross*].

147. Give a sketch of the administration of Oliver Cromwell and of his principal campaigns.   What share had he in the trial and death of Charles I. ?   Mention some particulars relating to these last mentioned events.   (1846, '49).

148. Mention the victories gained by Oliver Cromwell against his enemies abroad; and describe his foreign policy.   (1849, '76).

149. Give a brief history of the Protectorate of Oliver Cromwell.   (1857, '82).

150. What circumstances contributed to the speedy overthrow of the Protectorate ?   (1845).

151. Why was it not possible to maintain the Commonwealth in England after the death of Oliver Cromwell ?   What events led to the Restoration of the Monarchy ?   (1884).

152. Trace, from the death of Cromwell, the course of events which made Charles II. King of England.   (1847, '62, '70, '75, '77, '78).

153. What was the purport of King Charles the Second's Declaration at Breda ?   (1875).

154. What was the Cabal ? and with what policy were its members identified ?   (1871).

PRINCIPAL EVENTS. 15

155. In whose reign was the "Triple Alliance" formed? By whom was it chiefly brought about? Who were the parties to it, and what were its objects? (1853, '56, '84).

156. What was the Treaty of Dover in the reign of Charles II., and who were the parties to it? (1853, '76, '78, '84).

157. State briefly the parts taken by the Duke of Buckingham and Lord Shaftesbury in the reign of Charles II. down to the invention of the Popish Plot. (1876). [*Tait*].

158. By what Ministers was Charles II. successively governed? (1875).

159. Narrate the chief events in English History which arose out of the relations between England, France, and Holland, in the reign of Charles II. (1873). [*Hale*].

160. What was the date of the Fire of London? What were in this year the relations between England and other European Powers? (1883).

161. Give an account of the Rye-house Plot. (1854).

162. Relate the principal events in the reign of Charles II. (1851).

163. On what grounds did James II. quarrel with ✓the Bishops of the Church of England, and with what result? (1865, '77, '81).

164. What acts of James II. led directly to the loss of his crown? Describe the manner in which the Revolution of 1688 was effected. (1848, '51, '57, '65, '67, '71, '82, '83).

165. What were the immediate causes of (1) the Restoration, and (2) the Revolution of 1688? (1850).

166. Illustrate by reference to events of his reign the home policy of James II. (1883). [*Tait*].

167. Give, without detail, a list of the chief events in the reign of James II. (1854, '66, '72).

168. Relate the circumstances of the accession of William III. (1873, '83).

169. What were the difficulties against which William III. had to contend on his accession to the throne of England? (1876).

170. How were the great questions by which this nation was agitated during the Stuart reigns settled at the accession of William and Mary? (1879).

171. What measures were adopted by William III. for conciliating Scotland? (1875).

172. Give an account of the circumstances connected with the "Massacre of Glencoe." To what extent can blame be imputed to William in that affair? (1856).

173. Give your estimate of the personal character of William III. (1880). [*Ross*].

174. What were the relations of England, in the latter half of the Seventeenth Century, to Holland? (1873).

175. What was the substance of the Mise of Amiens, the Mise of Lewes, and the Dictum of Kenilworth? (1882).

176. Give a brief narrative of the chief events in the reign of John, or that of James I. (1870).

177. Who were respectively the first Prince of Wales, the first Duke of Cornwall, and the first Knight of the Garter? (1866).

178. Take the reign of Edward I. or of Henry VII. Mention the most important events which occurred in it. (1872).

179. When did English Kings first assume, and when did they finally drop, the title of Kings of France? Sketch the successive phases of English rule in that country. (1880).

180. For what are the reigns of the sovereigns who filled the throne in 1566 and 1365 respectively remarkable? (1866).

181. " During the hundred and sixty years which preceded the union of the Roses, nine Kings reigned in England. Six of these nine Kings were deposed. Five lost their lives as well as their crowns." (Macaulay). Give a list of these nine Kings, and mention briefly the circumstances which led to the deposition of the six. (1853).

182. Describe the relations between England and Flanders in the reigns of Edward IV. and Richard III. (1882).

183. Give some account of the sufferings of the English Roman Catholics in the reigns of Elizabeth and James I., and the causes of the Gunpowder Plot. (1882). [Green].

184. In what respects are the reigns of Henry III. and Charles I. alike ? (1860). [Ross].

185. Give a brief account of the Pilgrimage of Grace and of the Insurrection of Wat Tyler. (1864).

186. Characterise the foreign policy of Elizabeth and of Cromwell, and illustrate the opinion you express. (1867).

187. Give some account of the Puritans in the time of Elizabeth and James I. (1879). [Green].

188. What early Kings of England bore the following appellations respectively ?—Martyr, Ironside, Unready, Confessor, Harefoot. Give the dates and principal events of their several reigns. (1866).

189. What Kings bore the titles of Martyr, Confessor, Ironside, Harefoot, Rufus, Longshanks, Lackland and Conqueror ? Give the principal events in the reigns of the last two. (1867).

190. To what Kings of England, and on what grounds, have the following epithets been applied ?— The Peaceable, the English Justinian, Beauclerc, Longshanks, Bolingbroke. (1879).

191. Which of our English Sovereigns have been

c

personally engaged in War? Give particulars. (1870).

192. Give the dates and circumstances of the following events :—the Battle of Evesham; the death of Humphrey, Duke of Gloucester; the defeat of the Spanish Armada; the discovery of the Rye-House plot. (1858).

193. What historical events are associated with the names of Roger Mortimer and Owen Glendower? (1871).

194. Under what circumstances were Wales, Ireland and Scotland, united to England? (1868, '69).

195. Make a Chronological Table, as complete as you can, of the most important events of the 16th century. (1871).

196. What do you know of the Peace of Wedmore, the Declaration of Indulgence, the Habeas Corpus Act, the Treaty of Dover, the Toleration Act, the Peace of Bretigny, the Grand Remonstrance, the Self-denying Ordinance, the Statutes of Clarendon, Domesday Book. (1883).

197. Give an account of any remarkable popular Insurrections which occurred in the course of our history before the Stuart times. (1874).

198. Show at what periods and by what means the Naval strength of this country was more especially developed. (1875).

199. Explain and amplify this passage from Macaulay:—"The success of Henry II. or of Richard I. would have made England a province of France : the effect of the successes of Edward III. and Henry V. was to make France, for a time, a province of England." (1872).

200.
" For heaven's sake let us sit upon the ground,
And tell sad stories of the deaths of Kings,—
How some have been deposed, some slain in war,

Some haunted by the ghosts they have deposed,
Some poisoned by their wives, some sleeping
  killed,—
All murdered ; for within the hollow crown
That rounds the mortal temples of a King
Keeps Death his court."—*Shakespeare.*
Illustrate this passage, as far as you are able,
from English history. (1873).

201. Give some account of the trial and execution
of Lord William Russell and of Algernon Sidney.
(1884).

202. Name the Sovereigns who were reigning in
England at the close of each century from the ninth
to the eighteenth respectively. (1870).

203. Give the dates of the following events:—
The Accession of William I., Henry II., Henry IV.,
Henry VII., Elizabeth, James I., Charles I., Charles
II., and William III. (1878).

204. What were the principal events of English
History in the last twenty-five years of the 14th,
15th, 16th, and 17th centuries (1375-1400 A.D., &c.)
respectively ? (1863).

205. Arrange in chronological order, without comment or description, the chief events of the 16th
century, and give the date of each. (1862).

206. Say what events in history took place in
these years :—901, 1100, 1215, 1356, 1588, 1649,
1666, 1688. (1874).

207. What important events happened in English History in the following years :—937, 1166,
1304, 1360, 1461, 1513, 1628, 1645 ? (1880).

208. Describe the more important events that
were occurring in England in A.D. 827, 1066, 1265,
1346, 1535, 1648. (1868).

209. What important events were occurring in
England in A.D. 860, 1066, 1260, 1460, 1660? (1860).

II. Succession.

210. Under what circumstances did Egbert become king of all England ?   (1866).

211. Who succeeded to the throne of England on the death of Hardicanute ?   Explain the nature of his claims ; and illustrate by other examples in English History any apparent anomaly in the succession which took place on this occasion. (1865).

212. What was the nature of the claims of William the Conqueror to the Crown of England ?   How many and which of his sons succeeded him on the throne ? (1864, '76, '79). [*Freeman*].

213. What can be alleged in favour of king Stephen's claim to the throne ?   (1864).

214. On what grounds did Henry II. claim the crown ?   How did he proceed to strengthen its authority ? (1875, '76).

215. On what pretension was the claim of Edward III. to the crown of France founded ? (1881).

216. Whom did Richard II. succeed ?   (1856).

217. On the death of Richard II. who was heir to the throne, and whence and how was his title derived ? (1879).

218. On what grounds and with what justice did Henry IV. lay claim to the throne of England ? (1866).

219. What was the claim of Henry IV. to the crown ?   How far was it justified by facts ? How was it lost by his grandson ? (1877).

220. What were the claims of Henry VII. to the English crown, and how did he obtain possession of it ?   Give a genealogical table of his descendants, specifying more particularly those who succeeded to the English throne, and adding the dates of the accession of each. (1855, '65, '75).

221. What was Henry VII.'s title to the throne, and how were its defects remedied? (1867).

222. By what titles did Henry VII. claim the crown of England? and which of them appears to rest on the best foundation? (1873).

223. How did James VI. of Scotland succeed to the English throne? Give a brief account of his character. (1853, '64, '74, '78).

224. By what right did James I. come to the throne? How had the succession been determined in the case of each sovereign since the death of Edward IV.? (1877).

225. By what right did James I. ascend the throne of England? Who were his chief supporters? Who opposed his accession? (1879).

226. What were the chief incidents of the controversy in the reign of Charles II. as to the succession of the Duke of York? (1882). [*Green*].

227. Give a short account of the landing of William III. in England, and the steps taken by him and his adherents until his coronation. State also on what conditions he consented to take the crown. (1877). [*Macaulay*].

228. Under what circumstances did William and Mary come to the throne? (1880).

229. Mention the more important Anglo-Saxon kings, from Egbert to Edward the Confessor, assigning the exact or approximate dates to each. (1879).

230. Give a list of the Danish kings of England. (1853).

231. Show how Harold obtained the crown. On what did William of Normandy found his claims? (1858).

232. Name the English sovereigns, in order, of the House of Plantagenet. (1867).

233. Mention the names of the Plantagenet dy-

nasty.   What was their feudal relation to the crown
of France, and how did this relationship affect their
policy and conduct ?   (1878).

234. Enumerate, with dates, the English kings
from Richard II. to Henry VII.   (1857).

235. What were the several rights by virtue of
which the throne was claimed by the House of
Lancaster ?   (1880).

236. Give a list of the monarchs of the Tudor
family.   Describe briefly the character of each.
(1853, '68, '69, '79).

237. Give the names and dates of the Tudor
sovereigns.   To what circumstances were they indebted for their popularity, and the increase of the
royal authority ?   (1878).

238. Give, in their chronological order, the names
of the Tudor sovereigns, the dates of their accession,
and what you consider to be the leading events in
the reign of each of them.   (1876).

239. State when and how the Saxon and Norman
Lines merged in one sovereign ;   also when and how
the Lines of York and Lancaster.   (1863).

240. Name the principal kings of the family of
Plantagenet, of Tudor, and of Stuart.   By what
title did each family come to the throne ?   (1866).

241. Name, with dates, the kings of England,
from William I. to James I. ; and state in which
cases their title to the throne was defective.
(1860).

242. Explain the nature of the rights by which
Stephen, Henry VII., and William III., respectively,
came to the throne.   (1874).

243. Give the date, and tell briefly the immediate
cause, of each succession to the English throne from
the death of Henry IV. to the establishment of the
Tudors.   (1881).

244. Discuss the claims of Edward IV. and of

William III., respectively, to the throne of England. (1871).

245. Explain fully how the succession to the crown was ordinarily determined in England. Mention notable exceptions. (1868, '80).

246. Four times, at least, opposing claims to the Crown have been settled by the marriage of the claimants : state the facts. (1860).

247. What departures from the modern law of succession to the Crown may be noticed between William I. and Henry VII. ? (1869).

248. Name the English Kings from the time of the Conquest, who have either been deposed or have met with a violent death. (1880).

249. What instances are there in our history of the deposition of a reigning sovereign ? Date the event in each case. (1881).

III. Constitutional History and Laws.

250. What was the method of Government in Roman Britain ? Distinguish between *Municipium* and *Colonia*. (1870). [*Liddell*].

251. What Political and Legal Changes were introduced into this country by the Anglo-Saxons ? (1875). [*Creasy, Hallam, Hume*].

252. State what Laws and Customs were brought into Britain by the Angles and Saxons. (1852, '74, '78).

253. Give some account of the composition of the Witenagemot ; and also of the great Council of the Norman Kings. (1851, '81).

254. What is the Collection known as the Laws of Edward the Confessor ? (1868).

255. Discuss the Policy of Cnut. In what respects may that Policy be called Imperial ? What Laws is he supposed to have been the first to enact ? Explain their scope. (1879). [*Green, Lupton*].

256. Which English Kings, between Egbert and Harold, were famous as Law-givers ? State what you remember concerning the Legislation of any of them. (1881).

257. Give a short description of the mode of administering Justice in this country . before the Conquest. (1861). [*Hume*].

258. Contrast the position and power of the Crown in the Anglo-Saxon Constitution with that which it held in the early centuries after the Norman Conquest. (1885). [*Stubbs*].

259. With respect to the Anglo-Saxon Constitution, describe :—

    (1) The powers of, and rules of succession to, the Crown.

    (2) The powers and composition of the Witan.

(3) The machinery of local government. (1886). [*Creasy*].

260. Point out some differences between England before the Conquest, and England under the first Norman Kings, (*a*) in the way of making Laws, and (*b*) in the ways of administering Justice. (1873). [*Hume*].

261. What form of Government did William I. introduce into this Country? (1845).

262. What was William I.'s line of Policy with respect to the Church, and what were the Political Results of that Policy? (1844). [*Johnson*].

263. What innovations were introduced by the Norman Kings into the older systems of Legislation and Administration of Justice, as they existed among the Anglo-Saxons? (1877). [*Freeman*].

264. How did William the Conqueror provide in England for the maintenance of the Power of the Crown? (1881). [*Freeman*].

265. Point out the arbitrary character of the Government of the Anglo-Norman Kings. (1850).

266. What were the causes of the tyrannical nature of the Anglo-Norman Government, and the means by which its character was gradually altered? (1847).

267. What was the peculiarity of the Feudal System as established in England by William the Conqueror? Is there any instance on record, before the reign of John, in which the despotic power of the Sovereign was effectually resisted by the Barons? (1848, '49).

268. Mention some leading features of the Feudal System. When and through what causes did it decay? (1884, '85). [*Ross*].

269. What steps were taken by Henry II. to secure and enlarge the Royal Power, and to improve the Administration of Justice? (1876).

270. What were the Judicial Reforms introduced by Henry II. ? (1878, '79).

271. Describe the activity of Henry II. as a Lawgiver. (1882).

272. What is known as to the origin of Trial by Jury ? (1882).

273. What were the Constitutions of Clarendon? State their general purport; and the nature of the controversy out of which they arose. (1858, '79, '82).

274. Distinguish between the Constitutions of Clarendon and the Assize of Clarendon. In what years were they respectively confirmed ? (1865).

275. It has been said of the result of John's dispute with France, "Both the amount of what he lost, and the amount of what he retained, were important to the Constitutional History of England." Explain this statement, and justify it by a reference to the facts of the case. (1861). [Creasy].

276. Relate briefly the history, and state the most important provisions, of Magna Charta. How often was it ratified ? And what modifications did it undergo at successive ratifications? (1853, '56, '67, '72).

277. Under what circumstances was Magna Charta obtained ? Who were the principal leaders of the opposition to John ? What were the objects of the nobles and clergy, respectively, as shown by the provisions of the Act ? (1875, '76, '79).

278. State the leading provisions of Magna Charta and show that it is well entitled to be regarded as the grand foundation of English freedom. Does it contain the principle of the writ of Habeas Corpus ? If so, wherein consists the great value of the latter ? (1848).

279. Detail the circumstances which led to the ratification of Magna Charta by King John, and mention the dates of the meetings at Bury St. Edmund's and Runnymede. (1858).

280. Give the substance of the Provisions of Oxford. (1881, '82, '83).

281. Give a short account of the origin of the. House of Commons. (1849, '74, '83).

282. Describe the work of Montfort in regard to the Constitution of Parliament. (1885).

283. State the origin of popular representation in England, and trace the gradual progress of the authority of Parliament through the reigns of Edward III. and his successors, down to Henry VI. (1846).

284. Give a brief account of Edward I. in reference to the constitutional advances made in his reign. (1875, '77).

285. What were the Legislative Improvements introduced by Edward I. ? (1879).

286. Give some account of the relation of the English Baron to the Sovereign, before the close of the reign of Edward I. (1872). [Green].

287. How were the relations between the English Crown and Parliament affected by the French Wars? (1864). [Hallam].

288. Show what advance was made in the development of Parliamentary Government under the Lancastrian Kings. (1881). [Hallam].

289. What effect had, (1) the Wars of the Plantagenets with France, and (2) the Wars of the Roses, upon the Royal Prerogative ? (1849).

290. State the Limitations of the Royal Authority which existed at the accession of Henry VII. to the throne. How do you account for the high prerogative of his immediate successors? (1845, '47, '57, '65). [Hallam, E.].

291. Describe the relations between the Crown and the Nobility in the reign of Henry VII. (1881).

292. Give some account of the History of the Court of Star-Chamber. Why was it so called ? (1881).

293. Tell what you know of any statutes made before the reign of Henry VIII. for restraining the power of the Pope in England. (1883).

294. Take the reign of Edward I. or of Henry VII. Give an account of the chief legislative acts and changes which occurred in it. (1872).

295. What were the most important Laws enacted during the reigns of Henry VII. and Henry VIII.? (1870).

296. What were the principal measures concerning religion in the reign of Edward VI.? (1882).

297. What is meant by the Royal Supremacy? How was it developed under the Tudors? How was their policy in this respect favoured by the peculiar circumstances of the times? (1879). [*Creasy*].

298. Show the purpose and character of the Statute of Six Articles. (1868, '71).

299. What was the act of Uniformity? When, and in what circumstances, was it enacted? (1872).

300. What is supposed to have been the origin of the Court of Star-Chamber, and how was it remodelled during the reign of Henry VII.? By whom was the Court of High Commission created? Give instances of the manner in which the powers of these Courts were exercised in the reign of Charles I. (1856).

301. What were the origin and purpose of the Court of the Star-Chamber, and the Court of High Commission? When were they abolished, and for what reasons? (1852, '76).

302. What were the functions of the Star-Chamber, and of the Court of High Commission? Give some remarkable instances of the exercise of their power. (1862, '73).

303. Name the Principal Laws which were passed between the accession of Henry VII. and the death of Queen Elizabeth. (1852, '80).

304. How would you account for the degree of power exercised by the Crown in the reign of Henry VIII. and in that of Elizabeth? (1849).

305. What were the chief causes of the high prerogative of the sovereigns of the House of Tudor? Were the principles of religious liberty in any degree respected throughout their several reigns? (1845).

306. Point out the most remarkable epochs in the struggle between the Pontifical and Regal Power in England. (1846).

307. "Under the Plantagenets, Parliament had been an instrument of resistance, the guardian of private rights; under the Tudors, it became an instrument of government and general policy." State those historical facts which appear to you most strikingly to illustrate these statements. (1851).

308. State the chief principles of the British Constitution as it existed at the close of the seventeenth century, noticing the events which mainly contributed to the establishment of those principles severally. (1844).

309. State what you know as to the usages in force in the sixteenth century in regard to (1) imposing taxation, (2) legislation, (3) the preservation of the public peace, (4) the administration of the military power of the Kingdom. (1886).

310. Through what causes was the Influence of Parliament developed in the reign of James I., and that of his successor? (1878, '79).

311. Describe the doings of the Parliament which assembled in 1621. (1881).

312. Give instances of parliamentary opposition under Elizabeth and James I. State what was the subject of dispute in each case, and contrast their methods of dealing with the opposition. (1886). [*Hallam, E.; Ross*].

✓ 313. What gave rise to the Petition of Right, and what were its provisions?   (1853, '71, '72, '76, '84).

314. Describe any event of the year 1629 that has a prominent place in our Constitutional history. (1881).

315. By what unconstitutional means did Charles I. endeavour to raise money, and on what legal grounds, and with what justice did he defend those measures?   (1879).

316. Enumerate the principal measures of the Long Parliament in the order of their enactment. (1861, '78).

317. Against what grievances did the House of Commons protest in the reign of Charles I.? (1875).

318. What was the object of the Solemn League and Covenant?   By whom was it introduced, and with what results?   (1879).

319. What was the form of Government from the execution of Charles I. to the restoration of Charles II.?   (1864).

320. How was the government of the country carried on after the death of Charles I.?   What were the difficulties it had to encounter?   (1877).

321. What great advantage did the English Parliament, (as distinguished from similar bodies on the Continent,) possess in their long-protracted contest with the Crown?   (1851).

322.   Tell what you know of English Parliaments under the Commonwealth.   (1871).

323. What was the duration of the Long Parliament, and under what circumstances did it come to an end?   (1881).

324. It has been observed that the Long Parliament was three times supreme in the state, and three times dissolved in the midst of much indignation and derision.   Briefly describe the circumstances under which each of these events took place.   (1850).

325. Give some account of the Corporation Act, the Act of Uniformity (of Charles II.), the Conventicle Act, and the Five Mile Act. (1882).

326. What were the most important Acts of Parliament passed during the ten years succeeding the Restoration of Charles II.? (1872).

327. When was the Test Act passed? What was its object? (1853).

328. What gave rise to the Habeas Corpus Act? and what were its provisions? (1854, '71).

329. Name the chief statutes passed under the ministry of Lord Clarendon, and state the general effect. (1886).

330. What was the object of the Exclusion Bill? By whom was it promoted? and with what result? (1875).

331. Mention the chief Constitutional statutes passed in the reign of Charles II. (1855).

332. Give an account of the last four years of the reign of Charles II., with instances of an undue stretch of the prerogative during that time. (1886).

333. What were the causes of contention between James II. and the Bishops? In what way was James accused of violating the fundamental liberties of his subjects? (1877).

334. On what grounds was James II. accused of violating the Constitution? (1876).

335. What important modifications of the Constitution do we owe to the reign of Charles II., and to the Revolution of 1688? (1866).

336. Does any other event in the History of England admit of being compared, in its essential features, with the Revolution of 1688? State the grounds of your opinion. (1852).

337. What were the chief features in the settlement of our Constitution by the Revolution of 1688-9? (1884).

338. State the terms upon which William and Mary assumed the Crown, and show the Constitutional principles involved. (1886).

339. Give as clear an account as you can of the conditions associated with the settlement of the English Crown on William and Mary. (1883).

340. The criminal trials of the times of Charles II. and James II. are among the most discreditable in English History. Name any of them ; and state any changes in our judicial system, as to judges, juries, or laws of evidence, that originated in part with feelings these trials produced. (1860). [*Hume, Ross*].

341. The reign of the Stuarts has been called 'the age of good laws, but of bad administration.' Mention the good laws which we owe wholly, or in part, to their reign. Illustrate the second part of this statement. (1859).

342. Specify the advances made in Constitutional freedom from the Restoration to the Revolution in 1688. (1845). [*Creasy*].

343. What principles of importance were established by the settlement of William III. on the throne ? (1873).

344. What were the chief provisions of the Bill of Rights ? (1871, '72).

345. When were Triennial Parliaments instituted by law ? By what guarantees was the annual assembly of that body virtually secured ? (1865).

346. State and explain the chief provisions in the Act of Settlement. (1867, '79).

347. What were the most important legislative measures passed in the reign of William III. ? (1880).

348. What Constitutional struggles are connected with the following terms ?—The Constitutions of Clarendon; Benevolences ; Habeas Corpus ; and Immunity of Juries. (1864).

349. What right was specially secured by the *Confirmatio Chartarum* of Edward I. ? What rights by *Magna Charta*? (1860). [*Creasy*].

350. Give particulars respecting (*a*) Magna Charta, and (*b*) the Bill of Rights; and state the circumstances in which they were severally enacted. (1863).

351. State and point out the importance of the leading provisions of Magna Charta. Trace the gradual development of the authority of the House of Commons, from the period of its origin to the conclusion of the wars of the Plantagenets with France. (1850).

352. What were the Acts of Supremacy and Uniformity ? (1873).

353. Mention the main provisions of the Petition of Right, and of the Declaration of Rights ; and show how they contain a brief summary of the disputes between the Stuart Princes and their Parliaments. (1874).

354. Date, and state the substance of, the Covenant of 1638, the Self-Denying Ordinance, the Humble Petition and Advice. (1881).

355. State what you know of the Declaration of Rights, and the Habeas Corpus Act. (1880). [*Creasy, Hume*].

356. Give the dates and circumstances of each of the following incidents in the struggle which culminated in the Civil War :—The Petition of Right, Ship-money, the Solemn League and Covenant, the Grand Remonstrance, the Self-denying Ordinance. (1886).

357. What practices were condemned in the Petition of Right ? Explain the objects of the Grand Remonstrance. (1882).

358. Give some account of the Five Mile Act, and of James II.'s Declaration of Indulgence. (1871).

359. What were the following measures ?—The

D

Act of Uniformity, the Statute of Præmunire, the Exclusion Bill, the Six Articles, the Test and Corporation Acts. (1865).

360. State the fundamental principles of the British Constitution, and show how they are all either expressed or implied in Magna Charta, the Petition of Right, and the Bill of Rights. Give the dates of these three enactments. (1854).

361. Mention the chief provisions of the Test and Corporation, and of the Habeas Corpus, Acts, and give an account of the circumstances which led to their enactment. (1857).

362. Mention some of the earliest instances of a collision between the civil and ecclesiastical jurisdictions in England. (1865, '80).

363. Give an account of the leading disputes between the sovereigns of England and the clergy, from the time of Dunstan to the reign of Henry III. (1880). [*Ross*].

364. State briefly the relations of the Norman kings with the church, and their results on the sovereign and ecclesiastical power. (1879).

365. Give the principal features in the successive struggles between the Church and the Crown in the times of Lanfranc, Anselm, Becket, and Langton, respectively. (1885).

366. Name the most important laws affecting the relation of the Church and State before the time of the Reformation in England. (1871).

367. Name the chief acts of Parliament which affected the position of the Nonconformists in England during the latter half of the 17th century. (1874).

368. What statutes have limited ecclesiastical power in England? and what have limited the power of the crown? State the substance of each. (1867). [*Lupton*].

369. What Constitutional Questions were raised and settled in the reign of John, of Henry III., of Charles I., and William III. ? (1863).

370. What Constitutional Questions are connected with the names of Langton, A'Becket, " The Five Members," Lord Chancellor Shaftesbury, and " The Seven Bishops " ? Explain the importance of these questions. (1861).

371. What class of persons were the Barons who acted an important part in the reigns of King John and of Henry III. ? What places are associated in English History with the part thus acted ? (1864).

372. Our government is said to be a " system of checks." Explain and illustrate this statement. (1860).

373. Our government is generally described as a "Limited Monarchy." Explain exactly what this means. (1865).

374. What causes led to the aggrandisement of the royal authority under the Tudors ? and how did this affect their relations (1) with the nobles, (2) with the Church ? (1874).

375. At what time in our history has the prerogative of the sovereign been most extensive ? Give some notable instances of the exercises of that prerogative. (1872).

376. To what periods in our history would you point as those in which King, Lords, and Commons respectively, have been predominant, or have exercised unusual power ? (1865).

377. What is a Peer of Parliament ? Show in how many ways it is or ever has been possible for a person to obtain the dignity of a peerage ; and state precisely what are the functions of the House of Lords. (1862).

378. Describe in detail the powers, functions, and privileges of the House of Lords. (1872).

D 2

379. In whose reign, on what occasion, and with what results, were representatives for counties and towns first summoned to Parliament? How is it they were not summoned earlier? (1859, '64).

380. At what period of our history does the representation of the Commons become indisputably manifest? And when does it become quite clear that the *originating* power as to taxation was placed in their hands? (1848).

381. Sketch the progress of Popular Representation in England, from its commencement to the accession of Henry IV. (1878). [*Creasy*].

382. Note the successive landmarks in the progress of the increased influence of the House of Commons up to the end of this period. (1880).

383. What successive changes in Constitution has Parliament undergone? (1869).

384. What is an "Act of Parliament"? Describe the process by which, at any given period of our history, a proposed measure has been made into a law. (1863).

385. Explain the difference between an Impeachment and a Bill of Attainder. (1854).

386. Locke speaks of "the contract between the crown and the people." Does our Constitution recognise this term? To what discussion has it given rise? (1859).

387. Describe briefly in what ways taxes for the support of Government have been raised in England at different times. (1860).

388. Indicate briefly the most important facts in the history of Parliamentary Taxation. (1882).

389. 'The most marked progress in Constitutional Liberty in England was made under kings of weak personal character. Illustrate this statement by facts. (1860).

390. Distinguish between the executive, the judi-

cial, and the legislative, powers in a State, and mention the persons in whom these powers are vested by the British Constitution. Name also any remarkable occasions on which the Constitutional limits to any one of their functions have been overstepped. (1862).

891. Describe the origin of our Courts of Law, and the purpose of each. (1861).

892. To what facts in our history is it owing that the transfer of land is so much less easy than that of personal property? (1860).

893. What was the origin, and what the result, of the struggle between Henry II. and A'Becket, and between Charles I. and the Five Members? Mention any similar struggles between the Crown and its subjects—struggles that have had influence on our liberties. (1869).

IV. Social Institutions: Progress of Civilisation, etc.

394. Give a sketch of the manners and religion of the ancient Britons. (1852).

395. Describe some of the more important Institutions introduced into this country by the Anglo-Saxons. (1877).

396. Give a short account of the judicial system of the Anglo-Saxons. (1847).

397. What was the character of the religion of the Anglo-Saxons, and the state of feeling subsisting between them and the descendants of those whom they had subdued? Give proofs of the darkness in which their history, up to that time, is involved. (1850).

398. Give some account of the Anglo-Saxons, of their laws, manners and customs, religion, character and civilisation. (1884, '85).

399. "Learning followed in the train of Christianity. The poetry and eloquence of the Augustan age was assiduously studied in the Anglo-Saxon monasteries." (Macaulay). What monuments of the genius and learning of our Anglo-Saxon ancestors, of the period here referred to, remain to the present day? (1850).

400. Mention, in chronological order, the names of the most celebrated writers among the Anglo-Saxons, with a brief notice of the subjects of their respective works. (1847).

401. Describe the steps by which Christianity spread over England, and state the principal features of the Ecclesiastical organisation in the tenth century. (1885).

402. State the leading characteristics of the Normans and Saxons at the time of the Conquest. (1853).

403. Mention any facts that illustrate the state of England before the Conquest and after it. (1864).

404. Describe the Feudal System as established by William I. in this country. Are any approaches to that system discernible in the Saxon form of government? (1844, '73, '80).

405. In what respects did the Feudal System, as introduced into England at the Norman Conquest, differ from that which prevailed on the Continent? (1879). [*Johnson*].

406. What has been the influence of the Norman Conquest upon the language, character, and institutions of the English nation? (1855).

407. Describe the state of England, and the relations between the Normans and Saxons, during the first century after the Conquest. (1858).

408. Describe briefly the state of society under the Anglo-Norman kings. What circumstances were most favourable, and what most adverse, to the gradual progress of civilisation in this country? (1844).

409. To what agency would you mainly ascribe (1) the effacing of the distinction of the Norman and English races, and (2) the abolition of Villenage? Give your reasons in support of your opinion. (1849, '83).

410. Give a short account of the social and political condition of the English under (1) the Saxon, and (2) the Anglo-Norman, kings. (1846). [*Green, Hume*].

411. What was the effect of the Crusades upon the political and social condition of England? (1845, '68).

412. Illustrate the importance and the power of the Church in the thirteenth century. (1884).

413. What striking proofs did our ancestors afford under the Plantagenets of their zeal for learning, their commercial spirit, and their genius for architecture? (1852).

414. How long was the distinction between *Norman* and *Englishman* oppressively maintained by the Anglo-Norman kings? Show how powerfully the influence of the Church contributed to the effacing of this distinction, and also to the gradual abolition of slavery. (1850).

415. What do you know of the general condition of the Industrial classes in the Middle Ages? (1884). [*Green*].

416. State the effect of the Wars of the Roses (*a*) on the condition of the nobility, and (*b*) on the liberties of the people. (1886).

417. Trace the leading events and causes of the progress of liberty in England up to the period of the accession of Henry VII. (1852).

418. Give some account of the social and political condition of England in the reign of Henry VII. (1884).

419. Give some idea of the social condition of Elizabethan England. What provision was made for the poor? (1885).

420. What do you know as to the condition of the poor, and the laws especially concerning them, in the Tudor period? (1862, '63, '81). [*Ross*].

421. What circumstances led to the aggrandisement of the Gentry and Commons under the Tudors? How was it further augmented under James I.? (1876).

422. Mention as many facts as you can, to illustrate *the condition of the people* in the days of the Tudors and Stuarts. (1859).

423. What was the state of (1) Literature, (2) Science, and (3) the Fine Arts, in England in the reign of Charles II.? (1851).

424. Give some estimate of the Population of England at the death of Charles II., and say what were then the most important and populous English towns. (1870).

425. Trace the progress of English Commerce from the reign of Henry VII. to the commencement of that of William III. (1846).

426. When was the Royal Society founded? Name some of the most eminent men who belonged to it down to the reign of Anne. (1853).

427. What periods in the History of England, previously to the Revolution of 1688, were most favourable to (1) Literature, and (2) the extension of Commerce? Support your assertions by proofs. (1849).

428. What was the condition of England, as to population, wealth, political parties, and colonial settlements, on the accession of William III.? (1861).

429. Describe briefly the progress of English (1) Literature and (2) Commerce during the seventeenth century, carefully marking the dates in your answer. (1845, '61).

430. In what way were the potato, cotton, tea, and silk introduced into England? (1862).

431. By whom were Charters of Incorporation first granted to English towns? What periods, before the Revolution, were most favourable, and what most unfavourable, to the progress of Commerce? (1848).

432. During what period were the English most distinguished for their skill in Architecture? Support your assertion by proofs. What data have we for judging of the condition of the labouring classes in England, in the reigns of Edward III. and Henry VI.? (1846, '61).

433. What periods of our history are specially

remarkable for the introduction and improvement of manufactures ? (1862).

434. What eras in our History are most remarkable for the progress of Architecture and Commerce? When were most of our Colleges and Public Schools founded or enlarged ? Justify your answers by facts. (1859, '64).

435. Mention the periods in our History which are most remarkable for foreign discovery, adventure, or colonisation. (1865).

436. Name five of the principal events of English History ; and state briefly any facts that illustrate the influence of each on the condition of the *people*. (1860).

V. POLITICAL AND OTHER TERMS.

437. Give an account of the Witenagemote. Explain the Saxon terms Eorl, Thane, Ceorl, Tything, Reeve. (1854, '61).

438. What was the Saxon Heptarchy? (1883).

439. What is meant by the word "Heptarchy"? and how far is the current use of that word accurate? (1867, '71).

440. What is meant by Frankpledge, Escuage, Danelagh, Escheats, Gilds, Baronies by Tenure and by Summons? (1868).

441. Explain the words Duke, Thane, Count, Earl, Mayor, Alderman, Sheriff, Gild, Exchequer, and say to which of the peoples who have established themselves in Britain, they may respectively be traced. (1866, '80).

442. In what way, and by whose authority, are persons raised respectively to the rank of Judge, Peer, Sheriff, Knight of the Shire, Speaker of the House of Commons, Mayor, and Lord-Lieutenant? Say what are the chief duties required of the holders of these titles. (1873).

443. What was Domesday Book? and what is the meaning of the word Curfew? (1867).

444. Explain the meaning of the terms Fief, Tenant in Capite, Aid, Relief, Wardship. (1872).

445. What were the Crusades? (1862, '68).

446. With what facts or questions are the following names connected?—The Roman Wall, Domesday-Book, Frankpledge, Reliefs, Constitutions of Clarendon, The Dispensing Power. (1863).

447. Explain the terms Mortmain, Præmunire, and Ship-money. (1870).

448. Explain the meaning of the words Knights and Burgesses. (1874).

449. Explain the terms Baron, Peer, Vavasour, Tenure in Socage, Villein. (1882).

450. Explain the nature of Benevolences. When do we first hear of them? In what reigns were they most prevalent? By what monarch where they abolished, and by whom were they revived? (1865). [*Stubbs*].

451. Danegelt, Annates, Tallages, Poundage and Benevolences, occupy an important place in our History. Explain what they are, and give a brief history of each. (1859).

452. Who were the Lollards, the Jacobites, the Fifth Monarchy Men, and the Non-Jurors, respectively? (1870).

453. Give an account of Villenage; of the Law of the Six Articles; and of the Dispensing Power. (1866).

454. What *facts* are connected with the following names?—The Good Parliament; the Solemn League and Covenant; the Savoy Conferences; the Peace of Breda; the Bloody Circuit; Pride's Purge; Law of Six Articles; Perkin Warbeck; Offa's Dyke; Investiture; " Quia Emptores." (1879).

455. What facts are connected with the following names?—Bretwalda, Heptarchy, Heriots, Bocland, Duke, Alderman, Shirereeve, Danegeld, Villani. (1880).

456. Explain the origin of the words Homage, Socage, Tallage, and define their use under the Feudal System. Under the same system, what were the rights of Primer-seisin and Wardship? (1884).

457. Explain the following, and state what influence each has had on English History:—Interdicts and Provisions; Tallages, Subsidies, and Benevolences; Reliefs and Aids; Star Chamber and High

Commission Courts. Which represent Ecclesiastical struggles, which Civil, which Feudal? (1869).

458. What is meant by the Benedictine ·Rule? (1882).

459. What were the following, and what connection have they with English History?—Comes Litoris Saxonici; Friborg; Danegelt; Monopolies; The Trimmers; The Cabal; The Five Members; The Exclusion Bill; The Petition of Right; The Habeas Corpus Act. (1869).

460. Explain the term Lollards. (1881).

461. What is meant by the following terms?—The Royal Supremacy; The Court and the Country Party; The Fifth Monarchy Men; The Nonjurors; The Old Cause. (1877).

462. Explain the historical significance of these expressions:—The Court and Country Party; The Royal Prerogative; The Dispensing Power. How were they modified at the close of the 17th century? (1875).

463. Who were the Covenanters, Non-Conformists, and Non-Jurors in the 17th century? (1864, '79).

464. Define the term Puritan, and give some account down to 1620 of the party that went under the name. (1884).

465. Who and what were, respectively, the Lollards; the Committee of Safety; Colonel Pride's Purge; the Cabal; the Seven Bishops? (1867).

466. Who were the Pilgrim Fathers? Explain fully the terms Puritan, Nonconformist, Covenanter, Presbyterian, Independent. (1885).

467. What is meant by the Dispensing Power, and to what uses was it attempted by Charles II. and James II. to put it? (1882).

468. Explain the term Staple-Towns. (1882).

VI. ETHNOLOGY AND GENEALOGY.

469. What parts of Britain were inhabited by the Silures, Ordovices, Iceni and Trinobates ?   (1855).

470. What race inhabited the southern part of Britain when the Romans first landed in the country? (1855).

471. What do we gather from Caesar (1) respecting the races he found in Britain, (2) respecting their connexion with Gaul and Germany ?   (1880).

472. Describe the origin and character of the Saxon people ?   (1847).

473. What was the original home of the Anglo-Saxons ?   What parts of Britain did they occupy, and to what extent did they exterminate or expel the British race ?   (1855).

474. Who were the Normans?   (1845).

475. What was the original home of the Normans? (1855).

476. What monuments have we, architectural or literary, of the Britons, Saxons, and Normans in this island ?   (1862).

477. Mention the several populations out of which the English nation has been formed.   (1854).

478. Of what different races chiefly is the English nation composed?   Give the date of the introduction of each element.   (1860).

479. What separate races form the English people? State when each became incorporated.   (1869).

480. Give a genealogical table of the English kings from William I. to Henry II., adding the date of the accession of each.   Why is it said that the Saxon line was restored in the person of Henry II. ? (1855, '67).

481. How was Henry II. descended from Henry I. ? How many sons had Henry II.; and what became of them ? (1864).

482. Give a table of the children of Henry II. (1881).

483. From what country did the Plantagenet Princes spring ? How did the geographical position of that country affect their relations with France and England ? (1874).

484. Trace the descent from Edward III. of successive heads of the houses of York and Lancaster as far as it is necessary to explain their rival claims to the throne. (1881).

485. Give a full account of the lineal descendants of Edward III. who were living in the middle of the 15th century; and show that the claims of the House of York were really valid, according to the established law of succession to the English crown. (1858).

486. Give a table of the descendants of Edward III., so as to explain the Wars of the Roses. Give a table of the descendants of Henry VII., so as to explain the questions that arose, as to the title to the throne, after the death of Henry VIII. (1859).

487. Who was the mother of the Black Prince ? How was he related to John of Gaunt ? (1866).

488. Trace the descent from Henry III., of Richard II., and of each parent of Henry IV. (1881).

489. Whom did Cromwell marry ? What children had he, and what became of them ? (1880).

490. Show how the present Royal Family is connected with the House of Tudor—tracing the pedigree to the end of the 17th century. (1869).

VII. INVASIONS AND WARS.

491. Give a sketch of the gradual Conquest of
Britain by the Romans. Into how many provinces
was it divided by them ? Describe their respective
boundaries. Which of its towns enjoyed the privi-
leges of *coloniae*, and which of *municipia* ? (1847).
[*Ross*].
    492. Give the dates of Caesar's invasion of Britain.
How long did the Romans occupy this country ?
Mention the names of some of the more important
Roman commanders here, during that period ; and
state what were the advantages and disadvantages
of that occupation to the inhabitants. (1878).
    493. Give a brief account, with dates, of the
Roman conquests in Britain. Name the Roman
Emperors who died in Britain. (1853).
    494. What is the popular account of the settle-
ment here of the Angles, Saxons, and Jutes ?
(1878, '85).
    495. What is the date usually assigned to the
introduction of German tribes into Britain ? What
evidence is there to show that there were German
tribes in Britain before that time ? (1856).
    496. Under what circumstances, and at what
period, did the Saxons become masters of a large
part of Britain? (1847).
    497. Enumerate the successive settlements of
Saxons and Angles, giving the date of each immi-
gration ; and define the districts which they occupied. What does the name Mercia signify? (1858,'84).
    498. Give some account of the Conquest of Britain
by the English. When was Cornwall conquered ?
(1883).

499. State what is known of the successive Invasions of this country by races of Teutonic origin. What traces have we, in the names of places, of Danish settlements having been made here? (1868).

500. What. settlements of German populations are recorded in the early history of this country? From what quarters and at what dates did they come? (1880).

501. What circumstances hastened the consolidation of the Anglo-Saxon Conquest? (1877).

502. By which of the Anglo-Saxon Kings was the reduction of England under a single sovereign accomplished? (1851).

503. Who were the Danes? Give particulars respecting their incursions into this country; and show how far those incursions influenced the government, language, or manners of the Saxon people. (1862).

504. When did the Danes invade England; with what result; and to what causes did they owe their success? (1876).

505. Describe the effects of the invasion of this Island by the Danes, and the nature of the services rendered by King Alfred to his countrymen. (1850).

506. In what part of England did the Danes settle? (1853).

507. Describe, with dates, the Roman, Saxon, and Danish Invasions. (1868, '82).

508. What were the more important results of the Danish Invasions? How did they eventually help the national growth? (1885). [*Green*].

509. State briefly what is known of Invasions of Britain up to the time of the Norman Conquest. Give the facts in chronological order, and indicate whether the Invaders formed part of the English people. (1869).

E

510. Give the date of the Battle of Hastings, and relate the incidents that led to it. (1883).

511. At what period and under what circumstances did the Normans settle in France? Describe the character of that people. (1849).

512. Give the date of the Norman Conquest of England. (1855).

513. What circumstances facilitated the Norman Conquest, and by what circumstances was it impaired? (1850, '77).

514. Give a brief account of the Norman Conquest of England. (1853, '74, '75, '85).

515. What seem to you the most important results of the Norman Conquest? On the whole, should you call them good or bad for this country? (1883). [*Freeman*].

516. What King of England first acquired Guienne and Gascony; and how did he do so? In what part of France were those provinces? (1864).

517. Why was there a civil war in the reign of Stephen, and what were its chief events? (1882).

518. What Continental possessions had Henry II.? and how did he acquire them? (1867).

519. What were the foreign possessions of Henry II.? How far did he effect the conquest of Ireland? (1858).

520. Enumerate the dominions of Henry II. and state how they had been severally acquired by him. (1881, '84).

521. Describe the possessions of Henry II. when he came to the Crown, and his relations to France and England respectively. (1877).

522. Describe the Conquest of Ireland by Strongbow, and give an account of the chief risings against English rule in that Island down to the year 1650. (1880, '82). [*Collier, Lupton*].

523. When was England last invaded by a French Prince, and with what results ? (1860).

524. Give an account of the Barons' War, and its permanent political results. (1886).

525. Give some account of the Civil War in the time of Edward II. (1882).

526. What was the origin of the war with France in the reign of Edward III. ? Give a summary of the English wars in France from the time of Edward III. till the expulsion of the English from that country. (1857).

527. Give the principal incidents in the struggle between England and France under Edward III. (1885).

528. Tell what you know of Edward III.'s French Wars up to the Peace of Bretigny. (1882).

529. What were the two great Wars of Edward III. ? at what interval of time and place from each other where they fought, and with what results ? (1874).

530. What foreign dominions belonged to the Kings of England during the 11th, 12th, 13th and 14th centuries, and for how long ? How far did the possession of them affect the course of English History ? (1879).

531. In what Foreign Battles did the Black Prince play a conspicuous part ? and by what results were these battles followed ? (1866).

532. Specify the origin, duration, the most memorable events, and the final result, of the wars of the Plantagenets with France. (1845, '48).

533. At what time were our possessions in France of the largest extent ? How were they acquired ? How were they eventually lost ? (1883).

534. Give an outline of the course of the French wars from the reign of Edward III. to that of Henry V. (1886). [*Lupton*].

E 2

535. Mention the origin of the Wars of the Roses and also of the Plantagenets with France, and their respective consequences. Briefly notice the principal events by which they are severally distinguished. (1846).

536. What were the causes which led to the Wars of the Roses? Name the principal battles, with localities, dates, and results. (1857, '79, '85).

537. What was the origin of the Wars of the Roses; what their influence on the state of the nation? and how did they end? (1868, '71, '84, '85).

538. What is meant by the "Wars of the Roses"? Name in their order the battles in those wars, and state in what counties they took place. (1864).

539. In what foreign wars was England engaged during the time of Elizabeth? (1865).

540. Relate the story of the Spanish Armada. (1866, '80, '81, '83).

541. Date the Thirty Years' War. (1882).

542. Give a short account of the campaigns of Cromwell, and of his conduct in reference to the death of Charles I. (1852).

543. State the causes of the Civil War between Charles I. and his Parliament, and the principal events of that war. (1847, '85).

544. Name in order the places made memorable by their association with the struggle between Charles I. and his Parliament. Describe their geographical position; and say briefly what was the result of each battle. (1865, '71).

545. Enumerate, in order, the successive engagements between the Royal and Parliamentary Forces, giving the dates and mentioning the chief persons concerned in each. (1873, '78).

546. Give proofs of the power of England, and of its importance in the eyes of Europe, during the Commonwealth. (1851).

547. Date, and briefly account for the several Dutch Wars under the Commonwealth and Charles II. (1882).

548. Why did we quarrel with the Dutch in the reign of Charles II. ? Describe the course of the Dutch wars in that reign. (1881).

549. Tell the origin and course of the war, closed by the Treaty of Ryswick. (1873).

550. Give, with dates, an outline of the Conquest of Wales and of Ireland. (1864, '84).

551. Under what circumstances were Ireland, Wales, and Scotland either (a) conquered, or (b) made constituent parts of Great Britain? (1860).

552. Relate the circumstances attendant upon cne of the following events :—

(a) The Conquest of Wales by Edward I.

(b) William III.'s Campaign in Ireland.

(c) The Contest between the Civil and Ecclesiastical powers in the time of Henry II. (1862).

553. Give a brief account of the Wars with Scotland in the reign of Edward I., and with France in the reign of Edward III. (1868).

554. Tell the most important incidents in the Wars between England and Scotland during the rule of the first three Edwards. (1872).

555. Give a brief account of the wars between the English and Scotch in the reigns of Edward I. and Edward II. (1855).

556. Mention the dates and places when and where the Scots were signally defeated during the Tudor dynasty ; and with what results to the Scottish sovereigns and their subjects. (1877).

557. What Civil Wars have there been in England ? Give the dates, the occasions, and the results of them. (1864).

558. Give, with dates, but without detail, a list of Wars waged within bounds of England, Scotland,

*and Ireland, from the accession of William I. to the end of the Seventeenth Century. (1871).

559. What happened at the Battles of Lewes, Wakefield, Evesham, Crecy, and Naseby? (1874).

560. Give some account of the siege of Londonderry, the Battle of the Boyne, and the Massacre of Glencoe. (1873).

561. Of each of the following battles say when and why it was fought and how it ended:—Evesham, Falkirk, Bannockburn, Poictiers, Agincourt, Bosworth Field. (1873).

562. Among the 'decisive battles of the world' are reckoned the battle of Hastings and the fight at Orleans. Briefly state the circumstances and the results of each. To the last it has been said, we, as Englishmen, owe our freedom. Explain this statement. (1859).

563. Mention the dates of the following Battles and the circumstances under which each was fought:—the Battle of Lewes, of Stirling, of Shrewsbury, of Barnet, of Flodden, of Pinkie, and of Worcester. (1867).

564. Of each of the following battles—Lewes, Bosworth, Flodden, Naseby, and the Boyne—say why, and between whom, they were fought; and what was won for England by the victor. (1870).

565. Give the dates and relate the particulars of the following battles :—Edgehill, Marston Moor, Naseby. (1866).

566. Describe the battles of the Boyne and Steinkirk. (1858).

567. State the circumstances of the Battle of Shrewsbury, of Sedgemoor, of Dunbar, and of Cape la Hogue. (1861).

568. What were the results of the following battles?—Ethandune, Senlac, Sluys, Tewkesbury, Bosworth, Naseby, and Dunbar. (1878).

569. Of each of the following battles, say when it was fought, who were the combatants, and what was its result:—Lewes, Evesham, Falkirk, Bannockburn, Poictiers. (1881).

570. State particulars, with dates, of the battles of Lincoln, Evesham, Halidon Hill, Wakefield, Carberry Hill, Newbury, Zutphen, and La Hogue. (1869).

571. Mention six battles on English ground which exercised great influence on the history of the country. Give particulars of dates, places, combatants and results. (1869).

572. State between whom the following battles were respectively fought, and with what results :— Flodden; Najara; Halidon Hill; The Standard; Pinkie; Agincourt; St. Alban's; Neville's Cross; Towton; Naseby; La Hogue. (1867).

573. State what you know of the battle of Wakefield, of Pinkie, of Crecy, of Otterbourne, of Evesham, and of the battle of the Standard. (1863).

VIII. Biography of Eminent Persons.

574. Write a life of King Alfred. (1868).

575. Give a brief account of the personal character of King Alfred and of the results of his reign. (1875).

576. Write brief notices of the most distinguished Anglo-Saxon Kings and literary men. (1852).

577. Write the life of Cnut. (1879).

578. Give a brief sketch of the Sons of Henry II. (1867).

579. State what you know of the history of Thomas à Becket. (1865).

580. Who was Stephen Langton? Tell the Events in English History with which his name is associated. (1883).

581. Describe the career of Simon de Montfort. (1876).

582. Who was Simon de Montfort, and why has he been called the founder of the House of Commons? (1881).

583. Give a brief account of Edward I., and show, by reference to the events of his reign, how far he merited the popular title of " The English Justinian." (1877).

584. Describe the character and the policy of Edward I. (1883).

585. Sketch the life and reign of Edward III. (1869).

586. Write a life of Edward the Black Prince. (1880).

587. Who was the Black Prince? In what battles did he distinguish himself? In what part of Europe did they take place? (1864).

588. What eminent men were living in England at the time of Chaucer, and how were they severally distinguished? (1872).

589. What was the character of Henry VII.? (1855).

590. Give a short account of the personal history of Henry VII. to the Battle of Bosworth, and the date of this event. (1875).

591. Tell briefly the chief historical events associated with the life of Thomas Wolsey. (1881).

592. What different views have been taken of the character of Henry VIII.? Mention any facts that sustain the opinion which seems to you the most accurate. (1860).

593. Write a short life of Sir Thomas More, with dates. (1885).

594. Give some account of the life of Edward VI. (1871).

595. Mention the date and place of Cranmer's death. (1882).

596. Tell briefly the chief events in the life of Mary, Queen of Scots. (1881, '84).

597. Who was the Earl of Murray? (1882).

598. Mention the most distinguished writers, philosophers and statesmen, who lived in the reign of Elizabeth. (1856, '74).

599. Who was Edmund de la Pole? (1881).

600. What eminent writers were alive in 1587 in England, France, or Spain? and which of them were then generally known by their works? (1858).

601. Recount the chief incidents in the political life of Cecil, Lord Burleigh. (1872).

602. Give a brief account of the personal history of James I. before the death of Elizabeth. (1879).

603. Mention the names of the most considerable writers and statesmen that flourished in the reign of James I. (1854, '77).

604. What do you know concerning the political career of Buckingham after 1621 ?   (1881).

605. Name the most distinguished men who lived in the time of Charles I.; and write a brief life of any two of them.   (1861).

606. Narrate those passages of History with which the name of John Pym is especially connected. (1873).

607. Sketch the History of Thomas Wentworth, Earl of Strafford.   (1870).

608. Give a brief sketch of the Life of Charles I., from the incident at Holmby House to the imprisonment in Carisbrook Castle, giving accurately the dates and localities of the circumstances which you mention.   (1858).

609. Give some account of the political life of Oliver Cromwell.   (1872).

610. Tell—without entering into detail—the chie facts in the political life of the first Earl of Shaftesbury.   (1881).

611. Sketch the political career of James, Duke of Monmouth.   (1873).

612. Write a short history of William III., and an estimate of his character.   (1863).

613. Explain in detail, as far as time permits, the allusions contained in the following extracts :—

(*a*) " What murdered Wentworth, and what exiled Hyde,
By kings protected, and to kings allied ?
What but the wish indulged in courts to shine,
And power too great to keep or to resign ? "
—Johnson.

(*b*) " While Darwen stream with blood of Scots imbrued,
And Dunbar field resounds thy praises loud,
And Worcester's laureate wreath."*—Milton.*

(c) "Great Edward with the lilies on his brow
From haughty Gallia torn."—*Gray.*
(d) "Britain advanced and Europe's peace restored,
By Somer's counsels, and by Nassau's
sword."—*Addison.* (1861).
614. What Englishmen were illustrious in the
17th century; (a) as Historians; (b) as Statesmen;
and (c) as Warriors? Sketch the lives of any two
of them. (1868).
615. Give a short account of the literary labours of
Bede, Alcuin, and John surnamed Erigena. (1849).
616. What do you know about the following persons :—St. Augustine; Hereward; John of Gaunt;
The Earl of Essex; Fairfax; Bentinck? (1865).
617. What do we owe to Anselm, to Simon de
Montfort, and to William of Wykeham? Sketch the
life of Anselm and of De Montfort. (1867).
618. In whose reign did Geoffrey Chaucer and
John Wycliffe live? What services did they render
to English Literature? (1853).
619. Sketch the life of Lanfranc or of Archbishop
Anselm. (1878).
620. Write the life of one of the following persons :—Alfred; St. Dunstan; Edward the Confessor.
With what Scotch King was the latter contemporary?
(1867).
621. Mention the principal events in the life of
A'Becket and Wycliffe, of Bacon and Raleigh, of
Milton and Clarendon. (1860).
622. Write a short biographical sketch of *one* of
the following persons :—Alfred the Great, Wycliffe,
Sir W. Raleigh. (1861).
623. In what reigns did Lanfranc, John of Gaunt,
the Protector Somerset, Hampden, and Burleigh live
respectively? Write a short sketch of the life and
character of one of them. (1862).

624. Assign the following to their proper dates. and state for what each is remarkable:—Roger Bacon, Chaucer, William of Wykeham, Vandyck, Holbein, Caxton, Coke. (1863).

625. Give particulars respecting the following persons and the influence which they respectively exerted on English History:—Mary Queen of Scots, Cardinal Wolsey, Archbishop Laud, Joan of Arc. (1862).

626. Give some particulars respecting Sir John Oldcastle, William Penn, and Judge Jeffreys. (1870).

627. Who were Wat Tyler, Jack Cade, and the Nun of Kent? (1871).

628. Give some particulars respecting the life and doings of Bacon, Walsingham, Eliot, and Halifax. (1873).

629. Tell what you know of Lambert Simnel and Perkin Warbeck. (1873, '82).

630. State briefly who the following persons were, and what they did:—Anselm, Cranmer, Strafford, Monk. (1874).

631. State shortly what you know of Archbishop Morton, Thomas Cromwell, Earl of Essex, Lady Jane Grey, Archbishop Cranmer, Cardinal Pole, Lord Burleigh. (1885).

632. State briefly the chief facts in the political lives of Thomas Wolsey, Thomas Cromwell, and Thomas Cranmer. (1884).

633. Give some particulars respecting the life and actions of Archbishop Laud, Sir Thomas More, Sir Walter Raleigh, and William, Lord Russell. (1872).

634. Give a brief account of Cecil, Earl of Salisbury, and of the first Duke of Buckingham. (1878).

635. What events in English History are connected with Margaret of Anjou, John of Gaunt, Arabella Stuart, and Algernon Sidney? (1864).

636. Mention the principal events in the lives of Sir Francis Drake, Sir Thomas Overbury, and Earl Strafford. (1865).

637. Sketch the life of Sir Walter Raleigh and of John Milton. (1869).

638. What connection had Arabella Stuart and Lady Jane Grey with English History? (1866).

639. Give a brief account of the first Earl of Salisbury, of the Earl of Somerset, and of the Duke of Buckingham during the reign of James I. (1876).

640. State what you know of Arabella Stuart and Strafford respectively. (1868).

641. State what you know of the characters and careers of Danby, Sunderland, and Halifax. (1858).

642. Characterise the sovereigns of the Houses of Tudor and Stuart; and show how the characters of any two of them influenced the state of the nation. (1864).

B.—ROMAN HISTORY.

643. Explain what is meant by *domus Assarici*. (1885).

644. What is the probable origin, according to Niebuhr, of the legend of Romulus and Remus? With what king does he think that the purely mythic portion of Roman History terminates? (1845).

645. Mention the names of the Roman Kings, in the order which tradition assigns to them. (1877).

646. What reasons are there for believing that Rome, under her later kings, was the capital of a powerful state? Give a short account of the probable origin and nature of the Roman public land. (1845).

647. In what year is the last Roman king said to have been banished, and the Republic to have been established; and how long did the Republic last? (1877, '79).

648. Give a brief account of the internal history of Rome, from the expulsion of the Kings to the legislation of the decemvirs. (1853).

649. What campaigns established the supremacy of Rome in Italy? Give their dates, and state what remarkable men were engaged on both sides. (1873).

650. Who was the reputed progenitor of the family of the Claudii? and what character do, its members bear in Roman History? (1882).

651. What led to the exile of Coriolanus? (1882).

652. What was the extent of the Etruscan empire at the time of its greatest prosperity, and what was the general character of the Etruscan people? Name

some of the chief Etruscan towns besides Veii. (1881).

653. What was the first war, and what the last, between Etruria and Rome? When did Etruria become permanently an integral part of the Roman dominions? (1873).

654. " Majores vestri . . . . bis per secessionem armati Aventinum occupavere "; what events are here referred to? (1844).

655. Give the traditional account of the capture of Rome by the Gauls, and indicate the parts of it which are probably fabulous. (1881).

656. When was the *Dies Alliensis*? Give a brief account of the circumstances which gave the day its name. (1873).

657. Give a brief account of the Latin and Samnite Wars. (1866).

658. Name the chief battles fought by the Romans with the Samnites. (1873).

659. How did the Romans come into contact with Pyrrhus? By what generals, and in what part of Italy, was the contest with him carried on? (1871).

660. To what year is the foundation of Carthage usually ascribed? How does that date agree with the account given by Virgil? (1885).

661. Mention the most remarkable events which occurred in the first Punic War. Give a short account of the constitution of Carthage at that period. (1845, '75).

662. In what year did the first Punic War begin? and how? In what year did the last end? and who was the general of the conquerors? Mention any other celebrated commander of the same name. How were the two related to each other? (1861, '63).

663. Describe the terms of the Peace concluded between the Romans and Carthaginians at the end of the first Punic War. (1865).

664. Give a brief account, with dates, of the chief historical events between the first and second Punic Wars. (1865, '69).

665. Name in their chronological order the chief events of the second Punic War. (1844, '54, '64, '73, '74).

666. Mention the chief events, with dates, in the second Punic War, from the battle of the Trasimenus to the battle of Zama, both inclusive. (1865).

667. Give a brief account, with dates, of the chief historical events between the end of the second Punic War and the death of Caius Gracchus. (1865).

668. What view does Cicero in the "De Amicitia" take of the political action of Tiberius Gracchus ? Mention some considerations which might be urged on the other side.   (1884).

669. Mention the principal wars of Rome, from the end of the second Punic war to the Dictatorship of Sylla, with the date of each, and the names of the chief commanders.   (1864).

670. Give a sketch of the external advancement of the Roman empire, from the end of the second Punic war to the invasion of the Cimbri.   (1873).

671. Write briefly the history of Rome during the period occupied by the life of Terence, viz., from B.C. 195 to B.C. 159 ; and state what eminent men flourished as his contemporaries.   (1858).

672. Give the dates of the Macedonian Wars, with some account of King Perseus.   (1875).

673. Trace the gradual conquest of Macedonia by Rome.   (1874).

674. State the real or pretended origin of each of the Punic Wars, their respective consequences, and dates.   What ancient authors have given us an account of this portion of History ?   (1846).

675. Give the dates of the three Punic Wars, and

state the causes which led to the third, and its results. (1875).

676. A short account of the third Punic War. (1874).

677. The history of Roman Conquest in Greece. (1874).

678. Describe the site of Numantia, giving some account of its siege and the termination of it. On whom did it confer the title of *Numantinus*? (1872).

679. Give a short account of the origin, progress, and termination of the Numantian War. (1856).

680. Briefly narrate the history of the Kingdom of Numidia down to the time of the negotiations which preceded the Jugurthine War. (1880).

681. What was the origin of the war with Jugurtha? When and by whom was it concluded? (1872, '73, '76).

682. Describe the influence exerted on the progress of the Jugurthine War by Scaurus, Metellus, Sulla, and Marius; and give Sallust's opinion concerning the character of each of these persons. (1880).

683. What is known of the fate of Jugurtha? Where was he imprisoned at Rome? (1844).

684. Detail the circumstances which led immediately to the outbreak of the Marsic War. (1873).

685. Mention the most important events in the Civil Wars between Marius and Sulla. (1867).

686. Describe the effects of Sulla's proscription upon the proscribed citizens. (1884).

687. Relate the principal events in the History of Rome, from the termination of the war with Jugurtha to the death of Sulla. (1852).

688. Write a brief history of Rome from the termination of the Jugurthine War to the birth of C. Julius Caesar. (1860).

F

689. Trace the rise of the Kingdom of Pontus. In how many wars did Mithridates engage with Rome? Who were the generals that commanded in them, and with what results? (1871).

690. Give a brief account, with dates, of the wars against Mithridates. (1867, '76).

691. Recount the history of the conflicts between Rome and Mithridates to the time when the command was conferred on Pompeius. Describe the state of political parties in Rome at the time. (1880).

692. Give some account, with dates, of Pompey's war against the Pirates. (1870, '76).

693. Mention in chronological order the several wars in which Pompey was engaged, specifying those which are alluded to by Sallust in the Bellum Catilinarium. (1848).

694. In the speech "Pro Lege Manilia," § 28, it is said that Cn. Pompeius had served in "civile, Africanum, Transalpinum, Hispaniense, servile, navale bellum." Explain very briefly, with dates, what these wars were. (1880).

695. To what political party was Cicero inclined before he was made consul? What was the occasion of his speech against Rullus? What opinion does he express in that speech with regard to the principle of Agrarian Laws? (1848).

696. Give an account of Catiline's *two* conspiracies, with dates. (1848, '61, '75).

697. In what year was Catiline's conspiracy suppressed? and who were the consuls of that year? (1884).

698. To what class of citizens did most of the associates of Catiline belong? (1884).

699. At what time did the conspiracy of Catiline take place? What circumstances of the time gave the conspiracy its strength? State the measures taken by Cicero for its suppression. (1879, '84).

700. What was the conduct of Caesar in the affair of Catiline, and by what motives does he appear to have been influenced? What were the Clodian promulgations against Cicero, and their consequence? (1848).

701. Give some account of the chief towns of Gallia Cisalpina, and mention the historical circumstances connected with them. (1871).

702. What led Caesar to make war against the Helvetii? (1883).

703. What brought Caesar into conflict with the Germans under Ariovistus? (1883).

704. What provinces were under Caesar's administration during his Gallic war? (1879).

705. From what quarters did the Gauls receive assistance during their war with Caesar? (1879).

706. What do you think of Caesar's treatment of the Usipetes and Tenchteri? (1879).

707. Describe the position of Caesar in Gaul at the time at which B.G. v. begins. What were his powers? Whence were they derived? What part of the country was subject to his authority; and in what way had it been subjected? (1885).

708. When, and by whom, had the south of Gaul been conquered and constituted as a Roman province? (1883).

709. Give Caesar's account of the cause and origin of the Civil War. What time intervened between the crossing of the Rubicon and his assassination on the Ides of March? (1850).

710. What circumstances led to the Civil War between Pompey and Caesar? How far was their contest of the same nature as that between Marius and Sulla? (1871).

711. What special acts of his opponents induced Caesar to begin the Civil War against the party of the Optimates? (1879).

712. What provinces were assigned to Caesar after his consulship, and for how many years were they at first given to him ? (1883).

713. Give an account of the campaign of Crassus in Parthia. (1871).

714. Name the parties engaged in the battle of Pharsalia, and the events immediately resulting. (1872).

715. Relate the events between the battle of Pharsalus and the death of Julius Caesar. ‹1875).

716. Name the members of the two Triumvirates, and account for the unwonted union of power in each case. (1872).

717. Give a brief account, with dates, of the chief historical events between the death of Caius Julius Caesar and the battle of Actium. (1865).

718. Give the date of the Battle of Actium. What were the powers engaged in it, and what were its results ? (1882).

719. Describe the principal causes of the rupture between Octavian and M. Antony, both before and after the Treaty of Brundusium. (1870).

720. Point out the chief defects in the Roman Republic, and specify the causes of its dissolution. (1850).

721. When and for what reasons did Octavianus take the title of Augustus ? (1883).

722. What expeditions were undertaken by Augustus in the East, and with what objects in view ? (1877).

723. Name the first twelve Roman Emperors in their order, and give the history of the first and the last of the series. (1863).

724. Give the order of the first twelve Roman Emperors, with the date and manner of the death of each. State what was the relation of each to his predecessor, or, where there was no relation, the circumstances which led to his elevation. (1846).

725. Give the dates of the following events :—the battle of Zama, the capture of Corinth, the death of Tib. Gracchus, the death of Julius Caesar. (1853).

726. Give the dates, results, and geographical positions of the following battles :—the Allia, Cannae, the Metaurus, Zama, Cynoscephalae, Pharsalia, Munda, Philippi. (1859).

727. Mention the dates of the battles of Cannae, the Metaurus, Thapsus, and Actium, together with the parties engaged in them. (1876).

728. Mention the results of the battles of Pharsalia, Thapsus, Munda, Philippi, giving the dates of each. (1861).

729. Give the popularly received dates of the expulsion of the Kings from Rome, the establishment of the Decemvirate, the commencement of the first war with Carthage, the destruction of Corinth, the Social war, the death of Julius Caesar. (1862).

730. Give the dates of the capture of Rome by the Gauls, of the decemviral legislation, of the first plebeian consul, and of the death of Horace. (1877).

731. Give the dates and circumstances of the following events :—the taking of Rome by the Gauls, the battle of Cannae, the banishment of Cicero. (1858).

732. Give the dates of (a) the beginning of the Second Punic War ; (b) the death of Hannibal ; (c) the destruction of Carthage. (1868).

733. Give a brief account, with dates, of the following events :—the battle of the Allia, the defeat of the Teutones and Cimbri ; the introduction of the Publilian laws. (1860).

734. Write a concise account of the circumstances which led to the Wars of Mutina and Perusia, and their results; and give the site of these towns. (1870).

735. Write a brief *historical* commentary on this passage :—

Nosco crines incanaque menta
Regis Romani, primus qui legibus urbem
Fundabit, Curibus parvis et paupere terra
Missus in imperium magnum. Cur deinde subibit
Otia qui rumpet patriae, residesque movebit
Tullus in arma viros et iam desueta triumphis
Agmina. Quem iuxta sequitur iactantior Ancus,
Nunc quoque iam nimium gaudens popularibus
    auris. (1874).

736. What party in the state was headed by Appius Claudius ? Who were the Aerarii, and who was their leader, in the time of the Second Samnite War? (1868).

737. Who was Spurius Cassius ? What law was he the first to propose ? Describe the nature of that law. (1873, '78, '82).

738. Write briefly the life of M. Furius Camillus. (1881).

739. Give some account of Hannibal, and say who is alluded to as his conqueror in Hor. Od. iv. 8, and where and when he conquered him. (1877).

740. When did T. Quinctius Flamininus live, and what were his principal achievements ? (1879).

741. What was the relationship between Scipio Africanus Major and Scipio Africanus Minor ? Specify, with dates, the most important events in the life of each. (1862, '79).

742. What was the character of the younger Scipio, and what were the circumstances of his death ? (1884).

743. Give a brief account of the life of the younger Scipio. Quote the substance of the judgment passed by Cicero in the "De Amicitia" upon his life and character. (1880).

744. Give a brief account of the two Gracchi. (1866, '72, '74).

745. "Ti. Gracchus regnum occupare conatus est, vel regnavit is quidem paucos menses." (*De Am.* § 41). Discuss the justice of this remark by the light of historical facts. (1880).

746. The life and character of Marius. (1874, '75).

747. Write a short military biography of Sulla. (1873).

748. State, with dates, the chief incidents in Cicero's life. How did he spend the period of his exile? Mention the occasions of three or four of his principal orations besides those against Catiline. (1871).

749. Cicero's relations to contemporary politics. (1874).

750. The political relations between Cicero and Pompeius. (1874).

751. Sketch the chief events in the life of Caius Julius Caesar. (1861, '64, '65, '83).

752. The life and character of Sertorius. (1872, '74).

753. Give a sketch of the career of Lucius Licinius Lucullus. (1873).

754. Give a sketch of the career of Marcus Porcius Cato, together with Livy's estimate of his character. (1873, '79).

755. Explain the family connection between Julius Caesar and Augustus. (1878, '82, '85).

756. Write a short life of Virgil with dates. Comment on these words of Horace:—
"Forte epos acer
Ut nemo Varius ducit; molle atque facetum
Virgilio annuerunt gaudentes rure Camoenae."
(1874).

757. Explain the historical allusion in Virg. Ecl. I. 3, "Nos patriae fines et dulcia linquimus arva;" and state the probable motives which induced Virgil to compose the Georgics. (1870).

758. What was the state of affairs in Italy when Virgil composed his Georgics? What motive probably, and whose instigation, induced him to undertake the Poem? What internal evidence have we of the time when the first Georgic was written? (1873, '85).

759. Give the date of the birth of Sallust. What remarkable circumstances occurred in the year when he was tribune? Why are the generally received accounts respecting his moral character to be looked upon with suspicion? (1856).

760. Give a short account of the life of Sallust. What evidence is there to show that he belonged to a plebeian rather than a patrician family? (1848).

761. Give some account of the life and writings of Sallust, and mention a few prominent peculiarities of his literary style. (1880, '84).

762. Give a brief account, with dates, of the life of Sallust, the party to which he belonged, and his character as a citizen and a historian. (1871, '72).

763. What was the political and social condition of Rome at the time when Sallust wrote? Trace the causes, and state in chronological order the principal events of Roman History which happened between that period and the elevation of Augustus. (1848).

764. Does Sallust throw any light on the question of the early peopling of Africa? (1844).

765. Name the birthplace of Horace, the date of his birth, the profession of his father, and the principal friends and contemporaries whom he addresses in his writings. (1868).

766. In what war did Horace serve, and with what rank? Where was he when that war broke out? (1876).

767. What doctrine of Pythagoras is especially alluded to by Horace? (1876).

768. Why is Maecenas called by Horace *equitum decus* ? (1877).

769. Give a brief account of the life and works of Ovid, and the generally suggested cause of his exile. (1878, '81, '86).

770. What does Ovid himself mention as the cause of his banishment ? (1878).

771. What was the date of Ovid's exile? In what respects do the *Epistulae ex Ponto* differ from the *Tristia* ? (1883).

772. Mention one contemporary poet whom Ovid addresses in his Pontic Epistles, and state what kind of poetry he wrote. (1878).

773. Where and in what year did Ovid die ? (1878).

774. State what you know about Germanicus Caesar. (1878, '81).

775. Give a brief account of the following persons :—Marcus Porcius Cato the Censor ; T. Quinctius Flamininus; C. Marius ; Lucius Cornelius Lucullus. (1866, '67).

776. Relate one memorable event connected with the history of the following persons :—Fabricius; Appius Claudius the Censor ; Duilius ; Q. Fabius Maximus the Dictator ; Scipio Asiaticus ; and L. Mummius. (1867).

777. Arrange in chronological order and give the dates of the following persons and events:—Juvenal; Livy ; The First Decemvirate ; The Catilinarian Conspiracy ; The Third Mithridatic War ; Horace ; Pliny the Younger; Ennius ; The Samnite War ; Plautus ; Scipio Africanus Minor ; the Battles of Philippi, Cannae, Actium, and the Metaurus. (1869).

778. State very briefly the events or achievements which rendered the following persons remarkable, viz. :—Pyrrhus, Ennius, Fabius Cunctator, Fabricius Luscinus, C. Flaminius. (1879).

779. State what you know of Gaius Fabricius, M. Curius, and Ti. Coruncanius. (1880).

780. Explain any allusions which occur in the " De Amicitia " to C. Papirius Carbo, Sp. Cassius, L. Aemilius Paulus (Macedonicus), P. Sulpicius Rufus. (1880).

781. Give a brief account of the persons introduced as interlocutors in the Dialogue *De Amicitia*. (1876, '84).

782. State what you know about Parrhasius and Scopas. (1877).

783. Give a sketch of the career of Lucius Cornelius Cinna, or of Marcus Claudius Marcellus. (1871).

784. Mention briefly, with dates, some incidents in the lives and deaths of the two Catos. (1872).

785. Give a brief sketch of the lives of Marius and Sulla. (1863).

786. Describe the parts taken in the Jugurthine War by Marius, Sulla, Metellus, and Memmius. (1872).

787. Give some account of L. Lucullus and Q. Hortensius. (1876).

788. Give some account of Maecenas and of Marcus Vipsanius Agrippa, and their relations to Augustus. (1877, '82).

789. Explain :—
   (i) Aggeribus socer Alpinis atque arce Monoeci
       Descendens; gener adversis instructus Eois.
   (ii) Hic rem Romanam, magno turbante tumultu,
       Sistet, eques sternet Poenos Gallumque rebellem,
       Tertiaque arma patri suspendet capta Quirino. (1874).

790. Explain the allusions in the following extracts :—

(*a*) Quis autem est qui Tarquinium Superbum, qui Sp. Cassium, Sp. Maelium non oderit? (*Cic. Lael.* 28).

(*b*) Numne, si Coriolanus habuit amicos, ferre contra patriam arma illi cum Coriolano debuerunt? (*Cic. Lael.* 36).

(*c*) Dico te priore nocte venisse inter falcarios, in M. Laecae domum. (*Cic. in Cat.* I. 8). (1884).

791. Give (approximately) the dates at which these writers flourished, and say shortly what you know about them :—Catullus, Ennius, Lucilius, Lucretius, Plautus, Terence. (1874).

792. Give brief sketches of the lives of Cicero and Sallust. (1875).

793. Write down, in full, the names of Virgil and Horace. (1877).

794. How do you describe the three names of a Roman citizen, and what was their respective significance? How were slaves addressed? (1877).

795. What is the character of the *Claudia Gens* in the History of Rome? (1878).

796. Arrange, in chronological order, the Roman writers who flourished between 100 B.C. and 20 A.D.; and mention the principal works of each. (1872).

797. Name, with approximate dates, the principal writers of Roman History to the death of Augustus. (1872).

798. Who are the Latin Poets of the Augustan age, and what did they write? (1873, '77).

799. What is meant by *Laestrygonia amphora*? (1877).

800. Describe the institutions (1) social, (2) political, (3) military, ascribed to Romulus. (1873).

801. Explain briefly the division of the Roman citizens into *tribus, gentes,* and *curiae*. Distinguish

gentes maiores and *minores*, *patres* and *patricii*, *plebs* and *populus*. (1870).

802. The Italian communities under the government of Rome formed three main classes. State exactly the nature of each. (1873).

803. Why were the Roman people called *Quirites*? Is the term civil or military? (1877).

804. Explain the expression *Patres Conscripti*. (1875).

805. Mention the different names by which the patricians' are designated in the early books of Livy. (1874).

806. What was the original distinction between *Patres* and *Plebs*? Give the dates which mark the chief stages in the emancipation of the Plebs. (1874).

807. Mention, with dates, the chief legislative enactments by which the plebeians obtained political equality with the patricians. (1862, '71).

808. Give a concise sketch of the Servian Constitution, (*a*) in its military, (*b*) in its political, bearing. (1870, '74, '75).

809. Explain what is meant by *Belli portae*, and mention any occasions in Roman history on which they were closed. (1885).

810. Give a brief account of the three Comitia at Rome. (1854, '61, '68, '69).

811. For what different purposes were the Comitia Tributa held? What changes were made in them from the time of Julius Caesar to the reign of Tiberius? (1846).

812. What was the origin of the office of *Censor*? To what matters did his jurisdiction extend? (1871).

813. Who were the Curule Magistrates? Why were they so called? and when was each office instituted? (1863).

814. When, under what circumstances, and with what functions, was each of these offices created?—

Consulship, Praetorship, Quaestorship, Curule Aedileship. (1861, '66, '73, '74).

815. Describe the functions which belonged to the office of (1) *Consul*, (2) *Censor*, (3) *Curule Aedile*, (4) *Praetor urbanus* and *Praetor peregrinus*. (1875).

816. (i) *Tribuni militum consulari potestate*; (ii) *Praetor*; (iii) *Proconsul*; (iv) *Aediles Plebis*; (v) *Legati Caesaris*. When, and under what circumstances, was each of these offices instituted? (1872).

817. When were Military Tribunes with consular power first appointed, and when did they cease to be appointed? Mention the most important points in the history of this Magistracy. How were Dictators nominated? (1881).

818. Who were the *Tribuni militares consulari potestate*? When, and why, was the office created? When, and why, was it abolished? (1874).

819. Under what circumstances were the Tribuni Plebis first created? explain their *auxilium* and *intercessio*. (1869, '82).

820. What were the functions of the *Tribuni Plebis*? (1861, '82).

821. About what time was the office of Praetor first established? What jurisdiction had the Praetor Peregrinus? (1850).

822. Trace the history of the Praetorship. (1873).

823. Explain the term Legatus, Proconsul, Imperator. (1879).

824. What offices or duties did the Quaestors discharge at different periods? (1868).

825. What was the mode in which Consuls were elected at Rome? by what other names are they ever called? and what were their duties? (1862).

826. Trace the successive changes in the office of Consul, and describe the procedure at, and before, a Consular Election. (1873).

827. Give an account of the ceremonies attendant on the accession to office of a new Consul, to which allusion is made in Ov., Ex Ponto, iv., 4. (1881).

828. Give an account of the Censorship. (1867).

829. What were the duties and privileges of the Dictator, and what restriction was placed upon his power? (1871).

830. What is the number of Tribes said to have been instituted by Servius Tullius, and how were they divided? (1878).

831. State the circumstances which led to the enactment of the Laws of the Twelve Tables, and mention some of the chief provisions of that Code. (1874, '75).

832. Give an account of the reforms of Appius Claudius as Censor. (1873).

833. Explain the terms *Ferre, Promulgare, Rogare legem.* If a Roman law was called after the person who proposed it, from which of his names did it usually receive its title? Give instances from the "*Laelius.*" (1869).

834. Explain the difference between *Lex, Senatus consultum, Edictum.* (1874).

835. What custom is alluded to in the phrase *Primus instituit in forum versus agere cum populo?* (Cic., de Amicit. xxv). (1876).

836. What was the *album iudicum selectorum?* Mention the principal enactments which affected it. (1872).

837. Give some account of the Licinian Laws. (1872).

838. Explain what is meant by the *Lex de Sacerdotiis.* (Cic., de Amicit. xxv). (1876).

839. What was the purpose and what were the results of the Rogatio Mamilia? (1880).

840. State what you know about the Lex Porcia. (1875).

841. What was the object of the Plautian law, and when was it enacted ? (1848).

842. Describe the state of parties in Rome, and the circumstances attending the proposal of the Lex Mamilia. (1866).

843. Describe a Roman Legion and its divisions. What is meant by the Praetorium ? (1877).

844. Give a brief description of a Roman triumph. (1878).

845. What is the difference between *relegatio* and *exsilium* ? (1878).

846. Explain what is meant by *inquilinus civis*. (1875, '84).

847. What were the several degrees of *capitis deminutio* ? For what classes of offences was the penalty inflicted ? What was the corresponding penalty at Athens ? (1874).

848. What were the popular movements headed by members of the Licinian and Sempronian *gentes* respectively ? and what effect had they on the condition of the Roman Republic? (1873).

849. What were the leading principles of Julius Caesar's legislation ? (1873).

850. Explain the reform of the Roman Calendar by Julius Caesar. (1874).

851. What is the modern name of the month of Quinctilis, and what day of this month are the Idus? (1878).

852. The principal sources of Roman Revenue during the Republic. (1871).

853. Mention the various forms of Absolute Government, civil and military, which the Romans had submitted to, till the time of Augustus. (1872).

854. What was the special use to the Roman Emperor of the title of *Princeps Senatus*, of the Tribunitian Power, and of the Supreme Pontificate ? (1871).

855. What were the relations with Rome of (i) a

Colonia, (ii) a *Colonia Latina*, (iii) a *Municipium*, (iv) a *Foederata Civitas*?   (1872).

856. Write a short description of the mode of administering a Roman Province, as regarded both Justice and Revenue.   (1871).

857. Enumerate some of the principal Roman Provinces, distinguishing *Imperial* from *Senatorial*. (1877).

C.—GRECIAN HISTORY.

858. Can you assign any period, or give any crite-
rion, of the commencement of History as distinct
from Mythology? Name any of the earliest com-
posers of Greek History that occur to you. (1880).
859. Are any other Epic poems on Troy, besides
those of Homer, known to have existed? Give the
title and the supposed dates of any that you remember. (1878).
860. What are our sources of information respecting Homer? Upon what ground was he claimed by
the Athenians? What place has been assigned as the
most probable place of his birth, and for what reasons? (1844).
861. What inferences have been drawn (*a*) from
the mixed Aeolic, Ionic, and Attic words in Homer;
(*b*) from his general silence about the Dorians; (*c*)
from the mention of ἀοιδοί or bards; (*d*) from Δαναοί
and Ἀχαιοί as names for the Greeks? (1881).
862. What city appears to have the best claim to
being the birthplace of Homer? To what country
do the language, scenery, and natural phenomena
generally point? Does the poet show any know·
ledge of Hellenic Settlements in Italy? Mention
any that are supposed to be referred to in Odyssey,
Book x. (1869).
863. How long before the commencement of the
Olympiads is it most probable that Homer flourished? and how long before the age (1) of Lycurgus,
(2) of Pisistratus, and (3) of Herodotus? (1848).
864. What appears to you the most reasonable
account of the preservation and collection of the
Homeric Poems? Show, from various considerations,

G

the mighty influence which they exercised over the Grecian mind. (1850).

865. At what time are the Homeric poems commonly believed to have been composed? (1850, '83).

866. What are the grounds for believing that Homer was a blind bard who lived at Chios? (1879).

867. What are the grounds for believing that Homer was an Asiatic or Achaean poet? (1880).

868. What arguments have been alleged to establish the early date of Homer? (1877).

869. What meanings have been assigned to the name Ὅμηρος? What date is commonly given to the poet, and on what authority? What other poets were regarded by the ancients as contemporary? (1877).

870. Explain the names by which Homer designates the Greeks. (1883).

871. Illustrate Homer's account of the civilisation of the Phaeacians from the facts now ascertained with regard to pre-historic Greek culture. (1884).

872. State any theories that have been broached as to the date and authorship of the Iliad and Odyssey. (1875).

873. Show how the question of the date of the Homeric poems is affected by the fact that in them the Achaeans are represented as ruling in the Peloponnese. (1882).

874. What inference with regard to the origin of the Trojans may be drawn from the fact that the Homeric poems nowhere represent them as speaking in a different language from that of the Greeks? (1882).

875. State any reasons that have been advanced for thinking that the Odyssey came into existence at a different time from the Iliad, and in a different state of society. (1884).

876. Give some account of the political constitu-

tion of Greek communities, as depicted by Homer. (1882).

877. Describe the Government of Greece in the kingly period, as sketched in the Homeric poems. (1875).

878. Explain briefly the meanings of ῥαψῳδός, ἀοιδός, Ὁμηρίδαι. (1877).

879. What is known of the Schools of Homer in Ionic cities, and what do you understand by the term *Homeridae*? (1881).

880. To whom is the first collection and publication of the Homeric poems commonly ascribed? (1883).

881. What is related of Lycurgus, Solon and Pisistratus, in connection with the poems of Homer? What is the earliest date assigned to Lycurgus? Have we any trustworthy history of his legislation? (1879).

882. Of what Greek states is the history best known, and why? Point out the differing character of their governments at any period you may choose to select. Is any collective name given to the Greeks in the Homeric poems? How would the several cities be classified in the times which followed the Persian War? (1862).

883. What period is commonly assigned to the Aeolic Migration, and how far is the event historical or legendary? (1878).

884. What was the cause and proximate date of the Ionic Migration? In what part of Asia was the settlement effected? (1877).

885. What is the legend respecting the foundation of Tarentum? (1845).

886. Give an account of the conspiracies of Cylon and Cinadon. (1861).

887. Give the date of Pisistratus' tyranny, the names of his sons, the time and manner of their death, and the legend attributing to this family the introduction of the Homeric poems. (1869).

888. By whom was the Median Empire transferred to the Persians, and to which race did Cambyses and Astyages belong? (1881).

889. What three Dynasties of Lydian Kings are mentioned by historians? Which is mythic, and which historic? Give a summary of the History of Croesus as recorded by Herodotus. (1844).

890. Name the principal countries or dynasties overthrown by Cyrus the First. (1871).

891. Give a sketch of the life of Cyrus the Great. What was the duration of the Persian Empire? Relate those great events in its history which are immediately connected with the history of Greece. (1851).

892. By whom, and at what periods, was the city of Babylon captured? (1876).

893. By whom, and at what periods, was Babylon taken after Cyrus I.? (1881).

894. How many and what kings bore the name of Darius? (1881).

895. Give an account of the history of Corinth before the Persian War. (1872).

896. Give an account of the circumstances which led to the invasion of Greece by the Persians, and name any important states which took no part against the invader, with the reasons which were believed to keep them aloof. (1863).

897. Give a short account of the Persian invasions of Greece, dwelling upon the parts performed by the Athenians and Lacedaemonians, respectively, in preserving the liberties of their common country. (1848).

898. Mention the causes which led to the War between the Greeks and Persians. (1875).

899. What part of the great Persian Empire was occupied by the Persians proper and the Medes respectively? (1884).

900. Name the places and dates of the great Battles during the Persian War. (1875).

901. What were the circumstances which led to the revolt of Ionia from Darius ? (1871).

902. Give the date of the Second Persian Invasion of Attica. What happened to the city of Athens on that occasion ? (1879).

903. At what periods, and under what circumstances, were wars carried on against Aegina by the Athenians ? (1871).

904. The origin and political bearing of the Confederacy of Delos. (1874).

905. Between what contending parties, and at what period, was the Battle of the Eurymedon fought ? (1871).

906. Give a brief account of the Messenian Wars, and their results. (1875).

907. Write a short account of the Corcyrean sedition. Give the substance of the comments which Thucydides makes upon it. (1873).

908. Mention the most remarkable events which occurred in Greece between B.C. 500 and B.C. 400. (1852).

909. Sketch the relations between Persia and Greece from 478 to 401 B.C. (1873).

910. Give a brief analysis of Grecian history, with dates, from the Ionic revolt to the commencement of the Peloponnesian war. (1858).

911. Give a brief sketch of Grecian history from the end of the Persian Wars to the beginning of the Peloponnesian War. (1866, '68).

912. Give an account of the causes which led to the Peloponnesian War, and of the circumstances which preceded its outbreak. (1865).

913. Mention the causes of the Peloponnesian War, and the principal occurrences in it, with their dates. (1860, '74).

914. What were the chief sources of the Athenian revenue in the early period of the Peloponnesian War, and at the time when probably the Memorabilia was written ? (1849).

915. Mention some of the principal allies of Athens and of Sparta, respectively, in the Peloponnesian War. (1876).

916. Give the circumstances and date of the siege of Plataeae. (1872).

917. Give the circumstances and date of the revolt of Mitylene. (1874).

918. Give the circumstances and date of the capture of Sphacteria. (1872).

919. Give the circumstances and date of the battle of Delium. (1874).

920. Give the circumstances and date of the expedition of Brasidas to Thrace. (1872).

921. Why was the expedition to Sicily undertaken by the Athenians? Give some account of it. (1875).

922. Give the date, brief details and consequences of the battle of Arginusae, with its geographical site. (1871, '77).

923. What was the name of the naval battle which was fought between the Athenians and Peloponnesians a short time before the point at which Xenophon's History begins? What does Thucydides state as to its effect upon the Athenians ? (1855).

924. Trace the influence of Persia on the Peloponnesian War from 413 to 405 B.C. (1873).

925. Mention the most remarkable events of Grecian History between the point at which the History of Thucydides ends and the year in which the Anabasis took place. (1854).

926. What period intervened between the battle of Mantinea and the death of Alexander? Mention the most remarkable events which happened in it. (1844).

927. Relate briefly the circumstances (with date) under which Cyrus collected the Greek forces for the Expedition. Who was the Greek General who mainly promoted the scheme, and what induced Xenophon to join it ? (1879).

928. Give a brief account of Cyrus, and state the time of his reign. (1884).

929. Give the pedigree of Cyrus the elder from Cyaxares the First. Distinguish the parentage of Cyaxares II., Cambyses II., and Cyrus II. ; and give the name of the Athenian ruler who was contemporary with Cyrus I. To which Cyrus does Xenophon's Cyropaedia refer ? (1871).

930. Give the received dates of the death of Cyrus the elder and of Cyrus the younger. To which do the Κύρου παιδεία and the 'Ανάβασις respectively refer ? What was the relationship of Cyrus I. to Cyaxares ? (1881).

931. Give a brief account of the Cyrus of the Anabasis. What do you know of the ''Cyropaedia'' ? (1883).

932. Show some points in which the history of Cyrus given by Xenophon differs from that of Herodotus. (1881).

933. What do you know of Xenophon's life to the time of his joining the Expedition of Cyrus ? Name some works written by him in addition to the Anabasis. (1882).

934. What is the account which Xenophon gives of the circumstances which first brought him into contact with Cyrus the younger ? About what age was Xenophon when he joined Cyrus in Asia, and about what time did he die ? (1847).

935. What was the political situation of Greece at the time of the Expedition of Cyrus ? (1876).

936. How did Xenophon come to be one of the Greek commanders during the retreat of the Ten Thousand ? (1882).

937. Describe *briefly* how the Ten Thousand Greeks had come into the position in which they appear at the beginning of the third book of the Anabasis. (1886).

938. Give the history of the expedition of Cyrus up to the point at which the fourth book of the Anabasis opens. (1873).

939. Trace the retreat of the Greeks till they reached Trapezus. Give the modern name of this place. (1854).

940. What became of the survivors of the Ten Thousand after they reached the Hellespont? (1882).

941. Give an account of the history of Athens from the capture of the city by Lysander to the restoration of democracy. (1860).

942. What was the origin of the quarrel between Cyrus and Artaxerxes ? (1876).

943. Give some general account of the affairs in Asia which induced Agesilaus to make war against Persia. (1880).

944. State in chronological order the most remarkable events in Grecian History between the battle of Aegospotami and the Peace of Antalcidas. (1855).

945. Mention the most important events which occurred in Greece between the death of Lysander and the Peace of Antalcidas. (1857).

946. Give an account of the Peace of Antalcidas. (1866).

947. Mention some remarkable events in the life of Agesilaus which are mentioned in the Hellenics but omitted in the Agesilaus. How do you account for the omission ? (1857).

948. Give the circumstances and date of the battle of Leuctra. (1874).

949. Give a brief history of the Theban supremacy. (1872).

950. Give the circumstances and date of the battle of Amphipolis. (1872).

951. Mention some of the principal causes which paved the way for Philip of Macedon's progress to supremacy. (1874).

952. Write a sketch of Greek history, with dates, from the Peace of Antalcidas to the battle of Chaeronea. (1859).

953. Give a short account of the origin, progress, and fall of the Achaean League. (1872).

954. How long did the empire of Sparta last? Name the principal events which led to its overthrow. (1872).

955. Assign events to these dates B.C. :—559, 510, 500, 479, 445, 427, 422, 413, 411, 403, 394, 387. (1873).

956. Write down the dates of (1) the first Olympiad, (2) of the institution of Annual Archons, (3) of the beginning and the end of the Peloponnesian War. (1871).

957. Give some account of the following (a) Events:—Siege of Pylos, Battle of Arginusae, Peace of Antalcidas, Phocian War; (b) Persons:—Aristides, Cimon, Brasidas, Lysander; (c) Places:—Trapezus, Chalcedon, Himera, Thurii, Olynthus, Delium. (1863).

958. (a) Describe the results of the following battles:—Aegospotami, Leuctra, Mantinea (B.C. 342), Chaeronea (B.C. 338). (b) Mention the chief events in Grecian history, from the end of the Persian, to the beginning of the Peloponnesian, War. (c) Give an account of the constitution and history of the Amphictyonic Council. (1864).

959. Give the dates of the battle of Salamis, the destruction of the Long Walls of Athens, the death of Socrates, the death of Epaminondas, and the destruction of Thebes. (1865).

960. Give (1) the date, (2) the occasion, (3) the terms, of the conventions known as the " Peace of Antalcidas," the " Peace of Callias," the " Peace of Philocrates," the " Peace of Demades." (1873).

961. Give a brief account, with dates, of the following events :—the Thirty Years' Truce between Athens and Sparta ; the capture of Sphacteria ; the battle of Aegospotami ; the battle of Leuctra ; the peace of Antalcidas ; the battle of Chaeronea. Give an account of the Areiopagus and of the Council of Five Hundred at Athens, and of the Amphictyonic Council. (1860).

962. Give the dates of the following events :—(1) the Peace of Antalcidas ; (2) the Revolt of Mitylene ; (3) the death of Socrates ; (4) the Revolt of the Four Hundred. With what year of the Peloponnesian War does Xenophon begin his History ? (1870).

963. Give the dates and circumstances of the following battles :—Coronea, Cnidus, Mycale, Eurymedon. (1861).

964. Give the date of the battles of Marathon, Salamis, Plataeae, Aegospotami, Cunaxa, Chaeronea. Between whom were they severally fought? (1863).

965. Write down the dates of the following events, and mention the persons or states concerned in them :—

(a) Battle of Mycale.   (b) Taking of Naxos. (c) Revolt of Mitylene.   (d) Expulsion of the Thirty. (e) Seizure of the Cadmea. (f) Battle of Leuctra. (g) Destruction of Thebes. (1865).

966. Give the dates of, and name briefly the contending parties in, the battles of Arginusae, Corinth, Leuctra. (1869).

967. Mention the dates and most important results of the following battles :—Arginusae, Aegospotami, Coronea, Tanagra. (1870, '85).

968. Mention the dates of the great battles fought

at Marathon, Salamis, Plataeae, Leuctra, Sellasia, Chaeronea, and Leucopetra. (1874).

969. Give (in brief) the dates, localities, contending parties, and results, of the second battle of Coronea, and of that at Leuctra. (1880).

970. What are the legends about (1) Amphion and Zethus, and (2) Cadmus, founding the city of Thebes? What was the story of the Sphinx, and how was Oedipus connected with it? (1880).

971. Compare the character of the Athenians with that of the Spartans, and illustrate your statements by facts from their history. (1875).

972. To what cities did the following Τύραννοι severally belong, and when did they live? Cypselus, Clisthenes, Theron, Polycrates, Aristodemus, Jason. (1870).

973. Compare Brasidas, Lysander, and Agesilaus as representatives of Spartan policy. (1873).

974. Mention one important event in Grecian history, with its date, connected with each of the names of the following persons:—Solon, Pisistratus, Hippias, Clisthenes, Miltiades, Themistocles, Pausanias, Cimon, Pericles, Nicias, Alcibiades, Lysander, Epaminondas, Antalcidas, Timoleon. (1856).

975. Give a brief account of Themistocles, Cimon, Nicias, Brasidas, Lysander, and Pelopidas. (1865).

976. Give a brief account of the following persons:—Aristides, Pausanias, Pericles, Dionysius the Elder, and Epaminondas. (1865).

977. Give six important events in the life of each of the following persons:—Aristides, Cimon, Alcibiades, Pelopidas. (1867).

978. Describe some one important historical event in which Cimon was engaged; one in which Pericles was engaged; likewise one in which each of the following persons severally was engaged:—Archi-

damus, Gylippus, Mindarus, Lysander, Agesilaus, Pelopidas, Timoleon. (1868).

979. What eminent services did Pericles and Themistocles respectively render to their countrymen? (1845).

980. Describe some one particular historical event in which each of the following persons severally was engaged:—Brasidas, Iphicrates, Epaminondas, Alcibiades, Conon, Critias, Cleon. (1870).

981. State briefly what you know about Alcaeus and Sappho. (1876).

982. The life, character, and policy of Themistocles. (1873, '74).

983. The life and character of Cimon, son of Miltiades. (1873).

984. Give an account of the administration of Pericles, and state the year of his death. (1874).

985. What were the chief points in the foreign policy prescribed for Athens by Pericles? (1873).

986. Give an account of the family of Pericles and of the public affairs in which he took a prominent part. (1863).

987. State what is known of Prodicus. (1872).

988. Give a brief account of the historical events in which Brasidas and Nicias took a part. (1866).

989. Give a brief account of Theramenes. (1885).

990. What nickname was given to Theramenes, and why? How was his character estimated by the ancients? (1878).

991. What was the conduct pursued by Mithridates and Tissaphernes towards the Greeks? In what period of Athenian history, and in what way, did the latter take a conspicuous part? (1879).

992. Relate what is known of the history of Tissaphernes after the retreat of the Greeks. (1876).

993. Give a brief sketch of the life of Xenophon. (1874, '86).

994. What is known of Xenophon's life after the conclusion of the Expedition of the Ten Thousand ? (1883).

995. From occurrences narrated in Xen. Anab. iv., illustrate the qualifications of Xenophon as a commander. (1883).

996. Give the circumstances and date of the death of Socrates. (1867, '74).

997. Give a brief estimate of the character of Clearchus as sketched by Xenophon in Book ii. of the Anabasis. (1876).

998. Who was Archytas, and what is he celebrated for ? (1876, '82).

999. Give a brief sketch of the life of Conon, with dates. (1877).

1000. Give a sketch of the career of Agesilaus. (1872).

1001. What was the conduct of the Thebans towards Agesilaus, and how did he resent it ? (1880).

1002. Sketch the career of Epaminondas. (1875).

1003. The life and character of Pelopidas. (1872, '73).

1004. Relate the history of Timoleon. (1872).

1005. Relate the history of Dion of Syracuse. (1872).

1006. What public men at Athens are known as opponents of Demosthenes ? Have any of their orations come down to us ? and on what subject ? (1863).

1007. Write a short biography of Philopoemen. (1873).

1008. Who was Antiphon ? What part did he take in politics, and what was his fate ? (1878).

1009. Define the nature of the authority exercised by Ulysses at Ithaca, in so far as the Odyssey indicates it. (1875).

1010. To what extent was political freedom possessed by the labouring classes in Athens, Sparta, and Thessaly? (1870).

1011. Give a sketch of the changes in the government of Athens, from the earliest times to the beginning of the Peloponnesian War. (1861).

1012. Enumerate some of the principal changes in the Athenian Constitution, attributed to Theseus, and give the divisions of the people said to have existed in his time. (1871).

1013. What was the early political distribution of the people of Attica ? (1872).

1014. Give the date of Draco's legislation, and an account of its character. (1872).

1015. Give a brief account of the Athenian Constitution, from the time of Solon to that of Pericles inclusively. (1862).

1016. Describe and compare the Constitutions of Solon and Cleisthenes. (1872, '74).

1017. What were the reforms of Cleomenes at Sparta ? (1872).

1018. Give the legendary origin of the Court of the Areopagus, and the supposed reasons for the name. (1871).

1019. Give an account of the constitution of the Athenian *Boule* and *Ecclesia.* (1868, '85).

1020. Give a brief account of the site of, and a description of a popular meeting (*ecclesia*) in, the *Pnyx* at Athens. (1871).

1021. State, as accurately as you can, the method of proposing and passing laws at Athens. (1872).

1022. What is understood by the word "Amphictyony " ? What was its object? (1875).

1023. Give an account of the institution and influence of the Amphictyonies in Greece. (1872).

1024. To what Athenian statesman are the following Constitutional changes to be respectively attributed ?—(*a*) the establishment of the βούλη ; (*b*) the introduction of Universal suffrage ; (*c*) the organisation of the δικαστήσια. (1872).

1025. When was Ostracism instituted ? Explain its nature, and mention some of the principal occasions upon which it was used. (1873).

1026. What were the functions of the Archons at various periods of Greek History ? (1874).

1027. Relate briefly the rise and fall of the Four Hundred at Athens. (1872, '78).

1028. What was the object and the policy of the Thirty Tyrants ? (1878).

1029. How and by whom was Athens delivered from the tyranny of the Thirty ? (1885).

1030. The origin, constitution and functions of the Senate of Five Hundred at Athens. (1873).

1031. Sketch briefly the Spartan Constitution as settled by Lycurgus. (1870).

1032. Notice any distinctions that have been observed between βασιλεύς and ἄναξ as used in the Homeric poems. (1875).

1033. Describe the office of στρατηγός in the military system of Athens. (1876). .

1034. Define what is meant by the term ἁρμοστής. (1877).

1035. What is a πρόξενος ? (1874). ·

1036. What do you understand by a Laconian περίοικος ? (1874).

1037. Give some account of the principles and usages that prevailed in founding a Greek Colony ; and distinguish between ἔποικος, μέτοικος, and ἄποικος. (1871).

1038. Why was the Archonship of Eucleides regarded as an epoch in Athenian history ? (1861).

1039. Enumerate the principal writings of Xenophon. What sentiments does he appear to have held respecting the Spartan policy ? (1876).

1040. Why have doubts been expressed whether Xenophon was really the author of the Anabasis? (1883).

1041. What period of history does Xenophon embrace in the Hellenica? Can the work be regarded as a continuation of Thucydides? (1875).

1042. What period of Greek history is contained in the first book of Xenophon's Hellenics? With what year does it begin, and with what year does it end? (1877).

1043. Describe the condition of Athens during the period embraced by the first book of Xenophon's Hellenica. (1877).

1044. What reasons does Xenophon allege for the popularity on the part of the Spartans of Agesilaus' war against Persia? (1880).

1045. What was probably Xenophon's object in writing the Cyropaedia? Give reasons for believing it to be a genuine history or merely a political fable. (1847, '84).

1046. Name the chief Lyric Poets of Greece, and the times when they flourished. (1874).

D.—MODERN AND HISTORICAL GEO-GRAPHY.

1047. Define Geography. Into what two branches has it been divided? Specify fully the subjects held to be included in each branch. (1880).

1048. Enumerate and explain the different geographical names for particular conformations of land and water respectively. (1880).

1049. Define Latitude and Longitude. What is meant by the Antarctic circle? (1881).

1050. Define an *estuary*, a *delta*, a *creek*. Distinguish between *tidal waves* and *currents* in the ocean, and give some account of the Gulf-stream. (1882).

1051. What is meant by the "North-West Passage," "the Gulf-stream," "the Dark Continent," "the Roof of the World," "the Flowery Land"? (1884).

1052. Give some account of the Gulf-stream, the Trade Winds, and the Monsoons. (1882).

1053. Give some account of the chief currents of the ocean. (1884).

1054. Account for the geographical limits of the Trade Winds, and of the Monsoons. (1881).

1055. Name some districts that are nearly or altogether rainless, and others that have an excess of rain. Explain the cause of these conditions. (1880).

1056. What determines the course of rivers? Why is it that so few large rivers run westward? Trace the course of *one* of the following rivers from source to mouth, naming the districts traversed and the principal towns on either bank :—Danube, St. Lawrence, Loire, Shannon. (1879).

H

1057. Describe in words, or by the help of a Map, the configuration and the principal Mountain-systems of Europe. (1864, '75, '79).

1058. Give an outline of the Map of Europe, with principal Mountain-ranges and rivers. Insert British Settlements, and a dozen names of places connected with British history. (1863).

1059. Describe the range of the Little and Western Carpathian mountains. What provinces are bounded by them ? Name the rivers enclosed between their circuit and the Danube. (1877).

1060. Through or by what countries and cities does the Danube flow ? (1883).

1061. Sketch in outline a Map of Western Europe, insular and continental ; indicate the course of the principal rivers, and insert names of places remarkable in English History. (1866).

1062. Mention one principal river in each country of Europe; and state by what hills its course is regulated. (1869).

1063. Describe the Coast-line of Europe. What are the principal tributaries of the Baltic, the Adriatic, and the Caspian Seas ? Explain *precisely* the situation of the following places, and for what they are remarkable :—Naseby, Orleans, Fotheringay, Culloden, Fontevrault, Clarendon, Prestonpans, Kidderminster, Glencoe, Malplaquet, Wantage, Vinegar Hill, Utrecht. (1868).

1064. Enumerate six pre-eminently strong fortresses in Europe at the present day, mentioning to which state each of them belongs. (1882).

1065. Draw a Map of the Mediterranean, inserting in it the chief islands. (1876).

1066. Give some account of the Islands of the Mediterranean, and of the Peninsulas of Europe. (1880).

1067. Draw a Map of the eastern shores of the

Mediterranean, from the Dardanelles to Latakia. (1877).

1068. Draw a Map of the coast from Heligoland to the Bay of Biscay, marking the mouths of the rivers and the chief towns. (1876).

1069. Describe the coast (with maps) from Brest to Gibraltar, inserting the towns upon it, and shewing the rivers. (1878).

1070. Draw a Map of the country from the Eastern shores of the Black Sea to the Eastern shores of the Caspian, including the Volga provinces. (1878).

1071. Describe the possessions of the Turkish Empire. (1877).

1072. Sketch a tour by land from Lisbon to Rome, naming in their order the chief towns that might be visited, and the chief rivers and mountains that would be seen. (1873).

1073. A traveller passes from Smyrna to Gallipoli, thence to Odessa, and stops at Batoum. Describe the chief objects on his route. (1878).

1074. Give an Outline Map of France and England; insert three principal rivers in each country, the mountain-ranges, and the following places :— Tewkesbury, Edge-Hill, Crecy, and Toulouse. (1864).

1075. An exact description of the site of one, but not more than one, of these cities :—London, Paris, Madrid, Berlin, or Munich. (1878).

1076. Draw an Outline Map of the British Isles. (1874).

1077. Compare the coast-line of Great Britain with the coast-line of France, Holland, Denmark, and Norway. (1884).

1078. State the limits of the kingdoms of Northumbria and Mercia at the time of their greatest power. (1885).

1079. By what steps did the kingdom of Wessex

attain the supremacy amongst the Angle and Saxon
states?   (1885).

1080. Draw a Map of Britain with Roman and
Saxon divisions.   Insert the names of places where
invaders have landed.   Give the date of each invasion, and its results.   (1861, '69).

1081. Draw a Map of Britain, with Roman and
Saxon divisions.   Insert the principal rivers and
mountain-ranges;   York,   Carnarvon,   Winchester,
and Canterbury;   and state in order any important
facts connected with those towns.   (1861).

1082. Make a Map of Great Britain, marking in
it the English Counties.   (1883).

1083. Draw a Map of England.   Insert the following names, and explain each :—" Litus Saxoni-
cum," Northwic, Suthburh, the two " Mercias," the
two " Ham-tuns," Watling Street, and Foss Way.
Insert in the map the names of six towns of recent
origin.   (1860).

1084. How was this country divided, and what
were the most important towns in it, in the time of
the Saxon Kings?   (1874).

1085. What were the geographical limits of the
kingdom of Mercia?   (1858).

1086. Describe in words, or by the help of a Map,
the limits of the several Saxon kingdoms in England
before the time of Egbert.   Insert in your description the names of any towns which were of importance in that period.   (1863).

1087. Draw a Map (1) of Britain at the period of
the Danish Invasion; and (2) of that portion of
France which was subject to Henry II.   (1852).

1088: What were the great divisions of England
in the time of Edward the Confessor ?   (1868).

1089. Draw a Map of Great Britain, and insert
the names of a dozen places where important battles
have been fought;   add the dates of those that

decided the title to the throne. Insert also a dozen
names of Roman Municipia, Coloniae, and Civitates ;
and the principal Roman roads. (1859).

1090. Give the names and positions of the
English towns which had acquired importance previously to the Norman Conquest, and which continue
to the present day. (1851, '69).

1091. Draw a Map of the Southern and Eastern
Coasts of England, marking in it the estuaries and
the *chief* towns. (1878).

1092. Draw a Map of the British Isles, indicating
in it the distribution of the Mineral Wealth of the
country and the chief centres of Mining, Quarrying,
and Manufacturing operations. (1872).

1093. Give a Map of Great Britain ; mark the
position of the Mountain-chains, the Rivers on the
East Coast, and the principal Battlefields, with
dates. (1868).

1094. Which are the most widely wooded districts
in England ? State anything you know concerning
the extent of the great English Forests in earlier
times. (1881).

1095. Sketch an Outline Map of England ; mark
on it the boundaries of those counties which form
the line of the South Coast, from Ramsgate to
Land's End ; and indicate in each of them the
position of its most important towns. (1872).

1096. Sketch an Outline Map of England ; trace
on it the divisions of the Eastern Counties from the
Humber to the Thames, and mark the position of
their chief towns and rivers. (1873).

1097. Draw a Map of the South Coast of England,
from the Thames to the Severn, and of the opposite
Coast of France. Insert the names of as many
towns on both shores as you can ; and show the
limits of the Dukedom of Normandy at the time of
the battle of Hastings. (1861).

1098. Describe in words, or by the help of a Map, the entire East Coast of Great Britain, specifying as many details respecting towns, rivers, and inlets as you know. (1862).

1099. Name in their order the Shires whose coasts would be passed in sailing round England and Wales from Berwick to the Solway Firth. (1882).

1100. What are the great Estuaries on the East and West Coasts of England ? Mention the chief towns situated near them. (1877).

1101. Describe the position of these places, and say for what they are memorable :—The Boyne, Newbury, Lewes, Rouen, Dunbar, Runnymede, and Stamford Bridge. (1873).

1102. Mention any historical events connected with Eboracum. (1855).

1103. Describe the course of the Roman wall across the North of England. (1882).

1104. What memorable facts or persons are connected with Wantage, Winchester, Windsor, and Kenilworth ? (1867, '80).

1105. State the chief historical events connected with Yorkshire and Devon. (1867).

1106. What is the precise geographical position of each of the following places, and for what are they remarkable ?—Athelney, Bannockburn, Bloreheath, Dunbar, Verulam, Bosworth, Otterbourne. (1862).

1107. Describe the exact locality of these places : Bannockburn, St. Albans, Wakefield, Tewkesbury, Drogheda, Worcester, Copredy Bridge, Naseby ; stating for what events they are famous. (1876).

1108. A pedlar tramps from Penzance to Lincoln, or from Carlisle to Lincoln, by the shortest way, visiting as many towns as he can without adding much to the length of his journey. Take one only of his routes, the Southern or the Northern, and name in their order the chief towns through which he could pass. (1881).

1109. Where are Lewes, Evesham, Halidon Hill, ˙Neville's Cross, Otterbourne, St. Albans, Towton, Tewkesbury, Bosworth, Flodden? (1883).

1110. Name the county in which each of the following towns is situated, and state the chief industry and approximate population in the case of each town:—Blackburn,. Devizes, Durham, Oldham, Dundee, Ipswich, Leith, Maidstone, Dunstable, Lichfield, Plymouth, Montrose, Kidderminster, Hull, Leeds. (1886).

1111. Describe the position of these places, and state for what events in history they are famous:— Nottingham, Worcester, Newark, St. Albans, Gloucester, Marston Moor, Uxbridge, Edge-Hill, Newcastle, Culloden. (1877).

1112. Tell the geographical position of these Battle-fields: — Edge-Hill, Chalgrove, Newbury, Marston Moor, Naseby, and Preston. (1873).

1113. Name, in succession, the towns and villages rendered memorable by the events of the war between the Parliament and the Royalists; and say how each of them is situated. (1872).

1114. Name any eight places at or near which there was a conflict of troops in the civil war of Charles the First's reign, and tell what you can of their geographical position. (1882).

1115. Name any three of the principal rivers in England, with the towns situated on each; and show how physical circumstances have contributed to their importance. (1886).

1116. Draw a Map of the course of the river Thames, inserting the chief affluents. (1884).

1117. Describe the course of the Thames from its

source to the sea ; and compare it with that of the
Dee, and that of the Humber. (1875).

1118. Mention all the counties on the south of
the Thames and of the estuary of the Severn, and
the chief towns of each. (1875).

1119. A foreigner is making a journey from
Bristol to York. State through what counties and
towns he will pass, and some of the sights he will
see. (1874).

1120. Describe Yorkshire, with reference both to
its physical and political geography and adjacent
counties. (1871, '84).

1121. What points of resemblance or difference
occur to you between Cornwall and Lancashire ?
(1882).

1122. Sketch a Map of Lancashire, showing its
relation to adjacent counties, and marking the positions of its chief towns. (1870).

1123. Give an account of the geography of Yorkshire and Devon. (1867).

1124. Write a geographical description of any
county on the English coast. (1881).

1125. If lines were drawn through the greatest
breadth and length of England respectively, from
what points would they start, what distance would
they reach, what counties would they traverse, and
where would they intersect ? (1880).

1126. What were the principal maritime discover-
ies in the reign of Queen Elizabeth ? By whom
were they made ? (1868).

1127. Account for the first English occupation of
Virginia, and of New England. (1870).

1128. Draw a Map indicating the position of the
Battle-fields of the Civil War (1642—1651). Write
under the name of each place the date of the battle
there fought. (1865).

1129. Say which were the six most populous

towns in England in the time of Charles II., and
which six have the largest population now. Account, if you can, for the change. (1873).

1130. Enumerate the Colonies of England; say
when and how they have been acquired; and give
full particulars respecting any one of them of which
you know most. (1863, '72, '74).

1131. Name the most important British Colonies,
as nearly as you can in the order in which they have
been acquired; and give some particulars about the
population and resources of each. (1874).

1132. Put down, in chronological order, the most
important Colonial acquisitions made by this country
up to the end of the 17th century. (1880).

1133. What Colonies did England possess at the
end of the 17th century? When and how were they
severally acquired? (1866, '80).

1134. Name the principal British Colonies; describe their exact geographical position, name their
chief towns, and relate the circumstances under
which they were originally acquired. (1862).

1135. Describe the geographical lines followed by
English Colonial enterprise, and indicate the extent
of the field which it has covered down to the present
time. (1885).

1136. At what times were the following gained
for the British Crown:—The Channel Islands,
Orkney, Gibraltar, Malta, and Jamaica? (1885).

1137. Give as complete a list as you can of our
Foreign Possessions. (1885).

1138. Write a few notes upon English settlements
in America during the reigns of Elizabeth and
James I. (1882).

1139. Name and give the general direction of the
chief mountain courses of Scotland. (1886).

1140. Name, in their order, from north to south,
the chief towns, rivers, and bays on the west coast
of Ireland. (1872).

1141. Describe, or draw a Map of, the coast of Ireland from Bantry Bay to Donegal Bay, indicating the principal headlands, bays, and mouths of rivers. (1880).

1142. Of each of the following counties, say to what Province of Ireland it belongs:—Dublin, Cavan, Kilkenny, Cork, Meath, Tipperary, Down, Galway, Wicklow, Donegal, Sligo, Wexford, Waterford, Mayo, Londonderry. (1883).

1143. Name the four Irish Provinces. In which of these are Armagh, Cork, Drogheda, Sligo, Kilkenny, respectively, situated ? (1882).

1144. What counties in Great Britain and Ireland are at this day mainly inhabited by a Celtic population ? (1881).

1145. Where is the shortest distance between Ireland and Scotland ? (1866).

1146. Draw a Map of the respective possessions of Philip II. of France, and Henry II. of England at the death of the latter. (1874).

1147. Draw a Map of France, distinguishing clearly the several parts of its eastern boundary, and indicating the spots made memorable by the engagements in the Franco-German War. Insert the chief rivers and towns. (1871, '85).

1148. Mention the chief towns on the present frontier line between France and Germany. (1875).

1149. Name the chief rivers of Asia, saying of each of them into what sea it flows. (1882).

1150. Describe in detail two different routes to India ; and give reasons for preferring one to the other. (1873).

1151. Describe, in words, a voyage from England to India by the Suez Canal ; and mention the principal places of interest which would be passed on the way. (1870).

1152. Sketch a rough outline of the coast of

India, and show within it the relative positions of the Indus and the Ganges, of Delhi, Benares, Calcutta, Bombay, and Madras. (1884).

1153. Sketch an outline of British India, and mark in it the boundaries of the chief political divisions and the situation of the chief towns, rivers, and mountain-ranges. (1871, '73, '85).

1154. What are the great *natural* divisions of India? Give an accurate description of each. (1879).

1155. Describe the course of the Ganges; mention the provinces through which it runs, and the chief cities in its immediate vicinity. (1876).

1156. Give a description of the position of Afghanistan in the map of Asia. (1882).

1157. Describe different routes to Japan, and say which is the best, and why. (1874, '79).

1158. Describe the voyage of a ship from Calcutta to Japan. (1880).

1159. Draw a Map of Turkey in Asia, west of an imaginary line passing from Aleppo to Sinope. (1879).

1160. Draw a Map of British Burmah. (1886).

1161. What are the boundaries of Tonquin? of Tibet? of Turkestan? (1884).

1162. Mention the chief islands of the Malay Archipelago, and anything you know of any one of them. (1884).

1163. Give your notion of the extent and boundaries of the region called South Africa. (1881).

1164. Name the British Colonies in South Africa and the States bordering on them. (1886).

1165. Give some account of the climate and natural productions of Natal. (1884).

1166. Describe Egypt geographically. (1883).

1167. A native of Lancashire intends to settle in Chicago (Illinois). Describe his route from the

point he sets out from to the place of his arrival.
(1879).

1168. Sketch the geography of the great North
American lakes, and of the river St. Lawrence. (1881).

1169. Give some account of the geography of
British North America. (1872).

1170. A railway is to run from Montreal to Vancouver's Island, availing itself of the water-power
nearest its route.   Describe the lakes and rivers on
its line, and the chief obstacles it would have to
encounter from the physical conditions of the country through which it is to pass.   (1875).

1171. Name each of the United States of America,
and show, by a rough outline Map, their relative
positions.   (1871, '83).

1172. Describe the physical geography of the land
west of the Andes.   (1883).

1173. Name the countries that compose South
America.   (1885).

1174. Where are Teneriffe, Madeira, St. Helena,
the Gold Coast, Malta, Brindisi, Oude, the Punjaub,
Verona, Leyden, the Pruth, Santiago, and Avignon?
(1874).

1175. Of what states are the following towns the
capitals? — Stuttgart, Quito, Bankok, Bucharest,
Teheran, Lima, the Hague.   (1881).

1176. Describe the position of the Fiji Islands in
reference to Borneo, Auckland, Victoria, New Guinea,
and the Sandwich Islands.   (1875).

1177. Where are Sydney, Hobart Town, Adelaide,
Brisbane and Melbourne?   Where is the gulf of
Carpentaria?   Describe New Zealand.   (1873).

1178. Describe the geographical position of each
of the following places, and the events which made
it memorable:—Lewes, Naseby, Sedgemoor, Dunbar,
Towton, La Hogue, Londonderry, Stamford Bridge.
(1870).

1179. Describe the positions of the following places:—Widin, Jassy, Galatz, Kustendji, the two Scutari, Varna, Gallipoli, Salonika, Belgrade, and Temesvar. (1877).

1180. Tell, in a few words, the situation of each of these towns:—Antwerp, Amsterdam, Hamburg, Dantzic, Stockholm, St. Petersburg, Astrakan, Hyderabad, Bombay, Calcutta, Rio Janeiro. (1881).

1181. Describe accurately the situations of the following places, and state for what any of them are remarkable:—Liskeard, Bayeux, Jeddo, Presburg, Ryswick, Brest, Upsala, Crecy, Vancouver's Island, Ardres, Ajaccio, Fotheringay, British Columbia, Malabar, Surinam, Brindisi, Malplaquet, Runnymede, Ratisbon, Valetta, Monte Casino. (1880).

1182. Describe exactly the position of Rochelle, Agincourt, Nimeguen, Blenheim, Poitiers, Zutphen, the Tagus, Cape Breton, Lexington, and Boston. (1876).

1183. Describe the position of the following places:—Bannockburn, Bretigny, Poitiers, Bosworth, Pinkie, Marston Moor, Darien, Ripon, Breda, Senlac. (1876).

1184. Where are the following places, to whom do they belong, and for what are any of them remarkable?—Mocha, Merv, Sèvres, Cairo, Washington, Durban, Basle, Yokohama, Havana, Maritzburg, Tiflis, Assaye, Gravelotte, Dordrecht, Cette, Surinam, Quito, Andaman Islands, Kirkwall. (1880).

1185. Describe the situation of, and state the notable events connected with, the following:— Tewkesbury, Dunbar, Preston-pans, the Boyne, St. Albans, Marston Moor, Torbay, Pevensey, Battle Abbey, Edge-Hill. (1885).

1186. Where are Dunfermline, Kimbolton, Woodstock, Naseby, Drogheda, Runnymede, Donegal, Barmouth, Youghal, Haverford West? (1885).

1187. Where are Zanzibar, Owhyhee, San Francisco, Hobart Town, Heidelberg, Trebizond, Brisbane, Chicago, Herat, Ispahan ? (1883).

1188. Tell, as precisely as you can, the geographical position of each of the following towns :—St. Petersburg, Moscow, Copenhagen, Stockholm, Berlin, Vienna, Paris, Madrid, Lisbon, Constantinople. (1884).

1189. Describe the situation of the following places, either in words or by the help of a Map :— Finisterre, Utrecht, Dantzic, Runnymede, Beachy Head, Fotheringay, Wantage, Agincourt, Towton, Badajos, Malplaquet, Bayeux,- Stuttgart, Odessa. (1866).

1190. Explain in words, or by the help of a Map, the position of the following places :—Portsmouth, Rouen, Caen, Winchester, Lewes, the Seine, Hastings, the Medway, Havre, Calais, Rochester, Salisbury. (1865).

1191. Where are the following places and what renders them remarkable ?—Hexham, St. Albans, Dunbar, Rouen, Bannockburn, Drogheda, Colchester, Malplaquet, Naseby, and Dunkirk. (1863).

1192. Describe the position in relation to this island of the following places :—Spitzbergen, Greenland, Iceland, the Azores and the Canary Islands ;—and in relation to New York, of Newfoundland, Washington, and the Bermudas. (1875).

1193. Describe exactly the relative positions of these places :—Surat, Benares, Allahabad, Delhi, Mooltan, and Lahore. · (1879).

1194. What straits separate Ceylon, Sumatra, and Formosa, respectively, from the mainland? and what straits unite the Red Sea and the Persian Gulf respectively with the Arabian Sea ? (1879).

1195. Trace the course of the following rivers, and name the principal places on their banks :— Garonne, Shannon, Volga. (1866).

1196. Trace carefully in words, or by drawing a Map, the course of the Rhine, the Seine, or the Trent; and mention the places near which it passes. (1873).

1197. Name the chief town upon each of the following rivers :—Seine, Loire, Rhine, Elbe, Guadalquivir, Douro, Arno, Danube, Neva, Hudson, Mississippi. (1872).

1198. Describe the course of the following rivers :— the Rhine, the Danube, the Seine, and the Rhone ; mentioning the chief towns situated on the banks of each river. (1879, '86).

1199. Trace the course of the following rivers respectively :—the Danube, the Severn, the Garonne. Name in their order the towns on either bank from source to mouth. (1867).

1200. Trace in words, or by the help of a Map, the course of the Severn, the Thames, and the Seine —mentioning the districts through which they pass, and the towns upon their banks. (1862).

1201. Name the chief rivers which fall into the Atlantic, and one large town upon each. (1870).

1202. Sketch the coast passed by any ships of the Armada which started from Cadiz, and, after sailing through the North Sea were wrecked on the west of Scotland. Insert the names of rivers, both in Britain and on the continent, which empty themselves into the sea along the coast, and mark mountain-ranges. (1869).

1203. Describe accurately the site of the following battles :—Flodden, Najara, Halidon Hill, the Standard, Pinkie, Agincourt, St. Albans, Neville's Cross, Towton, Naseby, La Hogue. (1867).

E.—ROMAN GEOGRAPHY.

1204. Give some account of the physical structure of the peninsula of Italy. (1871, '75).

1205. What did the Romans understand by *Italia*? (1884).

1206. Draw a Map of ancient Italy, inserting the names of the chief political divisions, with at least twelve of the principal towns. (1853, '62).

1207. Draw a Map of Italy, and mark upon it the military roads and the towns which were situated upon them. (1863, '73).

1208. Draw a Map of Italy, marking the positions of the different provinces or districts into which it was divided by Augustus. (1882).

1209. What is the modern name of the Lucrine lake, and where is it situated? (1847).

1210. Give the ancient and modern names of the great lakes in Northern Italy. (1873).

1211. Give the ancient and modern names, and explain the course, of the chief rivers of Italy. (1855).

1212. Name the principal towns of Etruria. (1877).

1213. Draw a Map of Latium. (1858).

1214. Enumerate the seven hills of Rome. How far is Mount Aventine from the original site of the city? (1844).

1215. Mark on an outline Map of Rome, the Porta Collina, the Collis Quirinalis, the Mons Aventinus, the Capitolium, the Comitium, and the Mons Janiculus. (1881).

1216. Draw a Map of Rome, showing the relative positions of the Quirinal, Capitol, Palatine, and Aventine, the Forum Romanum, and the Campus

Martius. What part of Rome is believed to have been the earliest site of the city? (1870).

1217. Draw a rough Map of Rome in the age of Augustus. (1875).

1218. Describe the state and appearance of the Campagna di Roma in ancient and modern times. (1873).

1219. Give the names and mark the positions of a few of the principal towns and peoples near Rome said to have been conquered by Romulus. (1870).

1220. What were the boundaries of the Roman Empire in the time of Augustus? What is the present extent of the walls of Rome? (1849).

1221. Mention the distance of Tibur from Rome. What is it now called? For what is it famous? Give the names of other celebrated Grecian colonies in Italy. (1847).

1222. Describe the positions of the countries of the Aequians, Volscians, Hernicans, and Sabines. (1878, '82).

1223. Indicate, by Map or otherwise, the positions of Anxur, Algidus, Clusium, Allia, Ardea, Liparae, Massilia, Iuliae Alpes, Mediolanum. (1881).

1224. Mention the sites of Clusium, Ostia, Cumae, Corioli, Fidenae, Praeneste, Tusculum, and Lake Regillus. (1878).

1225. Mention the sites of the towns of Clusium, Tarquinii, Veii, Cumae, Circeii, Velitrae, Norba, Ostia; and the rivers that are tributaries to the Tiber. (1882).

1226. Explain clearly the positions of the following places :—Etruriae fauces, Praeneste, Comitium, Agrigentum, Cumae, Forum Aurelium, Tarentum. (1884).

1227. Define the position of Veii, the Trebia, the Trasimene Lake, Cannae, Perusia ; and give an account of the historical events connected with these names. (1867).

I

1228. Define accurately the positions of Ariminum, Vercellae, Placentia, Perusia, Beneventum, Cannae. (1867).

1229. What is the modern name of Tarentum? (1845).

1230. What events have occurred to alter the topography of the Cumaean region? Describe its aspect at the present day. (1849).

1231. Trace the course of the rivers Padus, Ticinus, Tiberis, Aufidus. Define the limits of Etruria, Umbria, Picenum, Apulia, Lucania, Bruttii. (1866).

1232. Indicate the line of the (1) Via Appia, (2) Via Aurelia, (3) Via Aemilia, (4) Via Flaminia; and name the chief place upon each. (1874, '83).

1233. Draw a Map of Magna Graecia. (1854).

1234. Define the sites of the most important cities of Magna Graecia, and give the dates and circumstances of their foundation. (1863, '66, '69, '73).

1235. Describe the principal passes across the Alps into Italy, giving their ancient and modern names. (1857).

1236. Draw an outline of the Alps known to the Romans as Alpes maritimae, Cottiae, Graiae, Penninae, Raeticae, Noricae; and fix the limits of each division. (1873).

1237. Draw a Map of the Rhenus or the Padus from its source to the sea, exhibiting its chief affluents and the countries through which it flows. (1873).

1238. Draw an outline Map of Sicily, marking the chief mountains, rivers, and towns, and particularly Lilybaeum, Syracuse, Ortygia, Cyane, Hybla, Eryx, Henna, Pelorum, Pachynus. (1881).

1239. Define the boundaries of Gallia Cisalpina. Why was it so called? Trace the course of the chief river of this province, with its affluents. (1863).

1240. Draw a Map of Cisalpine Gaul, marking the rivers and principal towns, with their ancient and modern names. (1860).

1241. Name and give the sites of six of the principal cities in Gallia Cisalpina, briefly noticing the historical events for which they were celebrated. (1872).

1242. Give the boundaries of Gallia Cisalpina. When was it made a Roman province? Mention the chief affluents of the Po, with their ancient and modern names, and the chief towns upon the banks of the Po. Mention and define the sites of the most important cities of Magna Graecia. (1861).

1243. Explain the geographical terms Gallia Cisalpina; Gallia Transpadana; Gallia Comata; Gallia Togata. Give the positions of Cannae, Tarentum, Patavium. (1868).

1244. Describe the boundaries of Gaul according to Caesar. (1883).

1245. Draw a rough Map of Gaul, to illustrate the Gallic wars of Julius Caesar. (1874).

1246. What part of Gaul was first conquered by the Romans, and at what time? (1879).

1247. Name the principal towns and rivers of Gaul spoken of by Caesar, and give their modern names. (1879).

1248. Assign boundaries to these divisions of Gaul:—(1) Provincia; (2) Aquitania; (3) Celtica; (4) Belgica. How was the map of Gaul altered by Augustus? (1874).

1249. Draw a rough Map showing how the country now called France was divided in the reign of Augustus; and notice briefly the principal stages in the conquest of the country by Rome. (1872).

1250. Mention the principal rivers of Gaul with their ancient and modern names, and describe their courses. (1883).

1251. Describe the position of the following:— Cassi, Remi, Eburones, Carnutes, Treveri, Cherusci, Trinobantes, Meldi. To what tribes did Lutetia,

Agendicum, Noviodunum, Durocortorum, belong? (1885).

1252. Who were the Allobroges? and why had they gone to Rome at the time of Catiline's conspiracy? (1884).

1253. Give the geographical position of Aedui, Nervii, Remi, Eburones, Treviri, Menapii, and the modern names of those regions. What was the position of Portus Itius, Samarobriva, Lutetia? (1864).

1254. Describe the course of the Rhone. Give the ancient and modern names of the chief towns upon it. (1874).

1255. Explain the expression, *lacus Lemannus, qui in flumen Rhodanum influit.* (1883).

1256. Show by a rough Map what was the course which Caesar took in crossing to Britain the second time. How far did he advance into the country? (1885).

1257. Draw a Map of that portion of Britain which was subject to the Romans—marking the positions of those towns which have acquired any historic celebrity in connexion either with the Roman or the Anglo-Saxon period—and giving their modern, as well as ancient, names, with a brief notice of the events by which they were severally distinguished. (1848, '49).

1258. Into how many provinces was Britain divided under the later emperors; and what were the boundaries and chief towns of Flavia Caesariensis? (1858).

1259. State the limits of Roman Britain (1) in the reign of Nero, (2) in the reign of Septimius Severus. (1854).

1260. What were the chief divisions of Britain, and their respective boundaries, at the close of the 6th century? Mention the Latin names of its principal towns and rivers. (1850).

1261. Give the ancient and modern names of the Roman colonies in Britain. (1855).

1262. Enumerate the chief Roman towns in Britain. (1857).

1263. Give the modern names of Mona, Vectis, and Eboracum. (1855).

1264. Define the limits and position of the Roman provinces of Achaia, Syria, Asia, Africa, Gallia Cisalpina. When, and under what circumstances, was each of these provinces formed? (1872, '73, '75).

1265. Mark on a Map of the coast-line of Spain the sites of the principal towns on or near the coast, and the mouths of the chief rivers, giving both the ancient and modern names of each. (1871).

1266. Draw a Map of Asia Minor, showing the territories into which it was divided at the time of the Mithridatic War. Mark on the map the position of the chief places mentioned in the course of the speech "Pro Lege Manilia." (1880).

1267. Describe (or draw in rough outline) the positions of Dacia, Maesia, Pannonia, Media, Parthia; and state the modern names of the territories with which they more or less coincide. Give in general terms the limits of the region which the ancients called " Scythia." (1868).

1268. Draw a Map of the northern part of Africa, tracing the limits of the various states as known to the Romans in the time of Sallust, and giving the modern as well as the ancient names. Point out the situation of the several places which are mentioned in Sallust's History of the War with Jugurtha. (1844, '52),

1269. Draw an outline Map of North Africa, marking Mauritania, M. Atlas, Numidia, Africa Proper, Libya, and the sites of Carthage and Cyrene. (1877).

1270. Indicate by means of an outline Map the principal territorial divisions of northern Africa as recognised by the Romans. What territory was included in the Roman province of Africa ? (1880).

1271. Describe the general physical character of, and mention some of the principal Greek Settlements on, the northern coast of Africa. (1872).

1272. Define the regions of Numidia, Mauritania, Gaetulia; and give some brief account of the Syrtes, the Tritonian Lake, and the Temple of Jupiter Ammon. (1872).

1273. Define the position of Numantia, Leptis (magna), Hippo (regius), Hadrumetum, Cyrene, Cirta, Utica, Zama, Thala, Carthago, Capsa. (1880).

1274. Where was Numantia situated? (1856).

1275. Explain the geographical position of the Kingdom of Pontus. (1876).

1276. What was the position of Tomi? Where did the Bistones live? What was the country of the Getae and Saurometae? Where was the Hister? (1881, '83).

1277. Describe the position of these places, and mention anything noteworthy connected with them:— Brundisium, Mutina, Numantia, Paestum, Pydna, Pergamus, Rhegium, Surrentum, Tarentum, Zama. (1874).

1278. The situation and importance of the following places :—Brundusium, Carthago Nova, Numantia, Tarentum, Verona. (1871).

1279. Describe the position of Praeneste, Etruriae Fauces, Seriphus, Gades, Forum Aurelium, Thermopylae. (1879).

1280. Describe the site, and state what you know, of the following places :—Faesulae, Capua, Tarracina, Carthage, Nuceria, Pons Mulvius. (1884).

1281. Describe the exact position of the following places, islands, and rivers, and give their modern names, when known :—Carthago Nova, Saguntum

Massilia, Messana, Lilybaeum, Mutina, Placentia, Melita, Aegates, Iberus, Isara, Druentia, Trebia, Ticinus. (1857).

1282. Define the courses of the following rivers:— Phasis, Halys, Anio, Enipeus, Apidanus, Caicus, Eridanus, Timavus. What were the geographical positions of Taenarum, Sila, Taburnus, Cytorus, Rhodope, Anxur ? Give the modern names of Patavium, Bononia, Perusia, Neapolis (Parthenopeia), Nauplia. (1860).

1283. What is the site of the following nations?— Allobroges, Ligures, Cantabri, Samnites, Rhaeti. Give the modern names of the countries they inhabited. (1863).

1284. Trace the march of Hannibal from Carthago Nova to the Trebia. Define the following geographical positions, giving the modern names, when known:—Carthago Nova; Iberus; Massilia; Rhodanus; Alpes Cottiae; Alpes Graiae; Alpes Penninae. (1865).

1285. Give the ancient names, and mark the geographical position, of the following places:—Marseilles; Lyons; Leyden; Brindisi; Tivoli; Cordova; Padua; Bologna; Constantinople; Cadiz; Messina; Carthagena. (1869).

1286. Indicate plainly the position, and make clear the political or commercial importance, of Samos, Delos, Misenum, Corinth, Numantia, Cumae, Agrigentum. (1880).

1287. Describe briefly the positions of Cnidus, Colophon, Cilicia, Pamphylia. (1876).

1288. Describe the positions of Sulmo, Tomi, Hybla, Paestum, Mounts Ossa and Pelion, and the Ceraunian rocks. (1878).

1289. Describe the positions of Gnosus, Pylos, and Gades. (1876).

1290. Describe the positions of the rivers Galae-

sus, Hydaspes, Phasis, Enipeus, Hypanis, Peneus.
(1877).

1291. Name the sites of Paestum, Tarentum,
Canopus, Pallene. (1877).

1292. Assign (*a*) Geographical position, (*b*) His-
torical associations, to Alesia, river Allia, Aquae
Sextiae, Asculum, Beneventum, Mutina, Pydna,
Sentinum. Thapsus, river Trebia, lake Trasimenus,
Veii and Zama. (1872).

1293. Where were the rivers Arnus, Athesis,
Baetis, Eridanus, Iberus, Arar, Liger,—the lakes
Ceresius, Fucinus, Trasimenus, Benacus, Larius,
Lemannus? and what are their modern names?
Derive the names of the following towns :—Bourges,
Brindisi, Cologne, Cordova, Lyons, Milan, Narbonne,
Naples, Otranto, Rimini, York. (1873).

1294. Set down (with their positions and modern
names) all the rivers which you remember as mentioned by Horace in connexion with Roman victories.
(1875).

1295. Give the modern names and the sites of the
rivers mentioned below : —

             " Phasimque Lycumque
Et caput unde altus primum se erumpit Enipeus,
Unde pater Tiberinus, et unde Aniena fluenta
Saxosumque sonans Hypanis Mysusque Caïcus."
Can the Eridanus be identified with any existing
river? (1870).

1296. Explain these references in Virgil :—

  (i) An mare quod *supra*, memorem, quodque al-
       luit *infra*?

  (ii) Iulia qua ponto longe sonat unda refuso.

  (iii)   Te, Lari maxime, teque
     Fluctibus et fremitu insurgens, Benace, marino.
(1874).

1297. Write a brief *geographical* commentary on these passages :—

(i)   Flerunt Rhodopeiac arces,
Altaque Pangea, et Rhesi Mavortia tellus,
Atque Getae, atque Hebrus, et Actias Orithyia.

(ii) Hi tibi Nomentum et Gabios urbemque Fi-
denam,
Hi Collatinas imponent montibus arces,
Pometios Castrumque Inui Bolamque Coram-
que.   (1874).

1298. What was the extent of the Roman Empire in the period comprised within the 39th book of Livy? What were the chief foreign powers, and in what relation did they stand to Rome? (1873).

1299. What was the furthest extent northwards, eastwards, and southwards of the Roman Empire at the time of the battle of Pharsalia? (1862).

1300. The extent of the Roman Empire at the death of Augustus. (1869).

F.—GRECIAN GEOGRAPHY.

1301. What ideas had the early Greeks about the shape of the earth, the course of the sun, and nature of the outer ocean ? (1880).

1302. What general idea of the world's shape had Homer ? Does he appear to have known Sicily, Phoenicia, Egypt, or the Euxine ? Which of the western (Ionian) isles does he describe ? (1877).

1303. What evidence is there in Hom. Od. ix., as to the range of Homer's knowledge of geography ? (1885).

1304. By what epithets does Homer describe the Hellespont, and how are these to be explained ? Mention any remarkable places on its shores, giving both ancient and modern names. (1862).

1305. What were the original settlements of the Doric and Hellenic peoples ? Does Homer mention them ? How does he use the term 'Αχαιοί ? (1880).

1306. What explanations have been suggested of the " Cimmerii living in darkness," and of the descent into Hades ? (1880).

1307. Draw a Map of the wanderings of Ulysses. (1846).

1308. How far is the geography of the wanderings of Odysseus imaginary ? (1884).

1309. Give a general description of the geography of the Troad. (1882).

1310. What are the chief views that have been put forward as to the site of Troy ? (1882).

1311. What is known of the commerce of the Mediterranean at the earliest time to which our knowledge extends ? (1884).

1312. When Greek writers speak of " the two Continents " which do they mean ? and how much was known in the fifth century B.C., as to the boundaries of these two Continents? (1874).

1313. Describe the Mountain-system of Greece Proper, and of the Peloponnese. (1872, '75).

1314. Mention any celebrated rivers in Greece, their direction, and any places of importance which stood on or near them. (1861, '74).

1315. Show how the geography of Greece tended to make the *Eastern* coast the front of the land. (1875).

1316. Mention and describe the situation of the most important plains in Greece. (1874).

1317. The position of the rivers Peneus, Strymon, Hebrus, Axius, Achelous. (1878).

1318. Name and give the site of the principal Inland Seas (or *inclosed* bays), and also of any *three* of the larger or more open gulfs in upper and lower Hellas. (1871).

1319. What were the boundaries of Greece? State its greatest length and greatest breadth. Trace the course, giving the names, of its chief mountain ranges. State the positions of Delphi, Thermopylae, Orchomenus, Megara, Sicyon, Megalopolis. (1860).

1320. Draw a Map of Greece south of Thermopylae, inserting about twelve of the most important cities. (1858).

1321. Draw a Map of ancient Greece, giving the modern as well as ancient names. (1845).

1322. Describe fully the physical features of Attica. (1875).

1323. Draw a rough plan of Athens in 450 B.C. (1873).

1324. Draw a plan of Athens with its harbours and environs. (1849, '72).

1325. Mention the principal states of Greece in the time of (i) Homer, and (ii) Aristotle. What were their respective forms of government at the later period referred to? (1846).

1326. Draw a Map indicating the positions of Aetolia, Phocis, Boeotia, Euboea, Attica, Corinthia, Achaia, and the principal towns in each country. (1852).

1327. Give the boundaries and describe the natural features of Laconia. During what period of Grecian history was Messenia included in the term "Laconia"? (1873).

1328. Describe the boundaries of Aetolia, and give the position of Leucadia, Cythera, and Corcyra. To what part of Italy does the last named lie most nearly opposite? (1871).

1329. Give the boundaries of Thessaly, Phocis, Achaia, Messenia, and of the Corinthian and Saronic gulfs. State the positions of Thasos, Delos, Cythera, and of Mounts Ossa, Oeta, Cyllene. Trace the course of the Peneus, Eurotas, Alpheus. (1860).

1330. What was the northern boundary of the Aegean, and what is its present name and political dependence? (1881).

1331. In marching from Athens to Actium, what States would be passed, and what Rivers crossed? (1870).

1332. Give a geographical description of Boeotia or Thrace. (1870).

1333. Name the sites of Mount Olympus, the river Enipeus, the island Scyros, and of Pylos, Orchomenos, Phthia, Iolcos. (1880).

1334. Describe the sites of the islands Aegina, Cythera, Ithaca, Leucadia, Cos, and Ceos. What group of islands were called the Cyclades, and why? (1878).

1335. Describe the geographical limits of Megara. When and how did it become an independent city? What were its chief colonies? What were its fortunes during the Peloponnesian war? (1872).

1336. State the geographical site of Ephesus,

Naxos, Corcyra, Phocaea, Samos, noticing any matter of interest connected with them. (1872).

1337. Fix the position of the following places, noticing any important historical incidents connected with them :—Amphipolis, Ephesus, Cyrene, Nemea, Potidaea, Samos, Tegea, Massilia, Decelea. (1874).

1338. State the geographical positions of Miletus, Thessalonica, Pherae, Chalcis, Sicyon, Melos, Massilia, Cyrene, Istria, Selinus, Megalopolis, Pella. (1875).

1339. Define geographically the promontories of Malea, Sunium, the Saronic, Maliac, Adramythian, and Issic gulfs; and the courses of the following rivers :—the Halys, the Eurotas, the Peneus and the Alpheus, the Strymon and the Boeotian Cephissus. (1861).

1340. Define the site of Pharsalia, Thapsus, Munda, Philippi. (1861).

1341. Define the positions of Plataeae, Mycale, Oenophyta, Aegospotami, Cnidus, Leuctra, Mantinea, Chaeronea. (1862).

1342. Where was Aulis ? what was the name of the nearest town to it ? why is the epithet Euboica given to it ? what is its bearing from Troy ? and what from Mycenae ? (1861).

1343. Where, and how situated, was Delphi ? Relate briefly some of the principal historical events with which it is associated. By what name is it mentioned in Homer ? (1871).

1344. What do you know of the Trees, or Fruits, or Flowers, that grow in different parts of Greece ? (1875).

1345. Describe the geographical position of the peninsula known in ancient times by the name of the Thracian Chersonese, and mention the names of the principal towns therein. (1853).

1346. By whom was the Chalcidic peninsula colonised? Mention the names of its chief towns and the important events in Grecian history with which they are associated. (1853).

1347. Fix the site of each of the following Greek colonies, and mention the time when, and the circumstances under which, each was founded :—Syracuse, Sybaris, Tarentum, Massilia, Cyrene, Corcyra, Potidaea. (1868).

1348. Where was Tarentum? and why is it called *Lacedaemonium?* Define the site of the chief cities in Magna Graecia. (1865).

1349. The history of the principal Greek Colonies in Thrace. (1872).

1350. The chief Colonies of Miletus, Megara, Chalcis, Corinth. (1874).

1351. Give the names, and describe the position, of some of the chief Greek Colonies in Asia Minor, and mention any memorable event associated with each. (1864).

1352. Mention the principal Colonies of the Greeks in Sicily, southern Italy, and Africa; with the dates of their foundation. (1875).

1353. Assign (1) mother city, (2) approximate date of foundation, (3) geographical position, to each of these Colonies:—Cumae, Syracuse, Agrigentum, Sybaris, Tarentum, Cyrene, Istria. (1873).

1354. Draw a sketch of the coast-line of Asia Minor, marking the principal islands and the positions of the chief towns. (1870).

1355. Draw a Map of the *general* shape of Asia Minor, with the principal outlying islands. (1877).

1356. Give some description (briefly) of the Plain of Troy, the rivers Scamander and Simois, and their relation to the supposed site of Ilium. (1881).

1357. Describe the position of Tenedos, Lemnos, and Imbros in respect of Troy. (1881).

1358. Give the names, and describe the general areas, of the different seas in the basin of the Mediterranean. (1879).

1359. Mark, on a Map of Sicily, the principal places which figure in the history of the Sicilian Expedition, distinguishing the cities of Doric and of Ionic origin. (1873).

1360. Draw an outline of the Black Sea, and fill up the coast with the names of the chief towns on it. (1872).

1361. Draw an outline of the Propontis, marking the Hellespont, Chersonesus, Cyzicus, Bosporus, Chalcedon, Byzantium. (1878).

1362. What were the limits of the Persian Empire at the period of its greatest extent? (1851).

1363. Draw a Map which shall include Sardis, Sinope, and the spot from whence the retreat of the Ten Thousand began. Trace on it, if you can, their route out, and their route back again. (1864).

1364. Name the principal towns mentioned by Xenophon along the course of the Tigris; and state what he says of the number of the population in that district. (1876).

1365. Draw a Map of Asia Minor. Trace the course of the Euphrates and the Tigris; and mark out the route of the Ten Thousand after the battle of Cunaxa. (1851, '84).

1366. Trace on a rough Map the line of the retreat from the Καρδούχια ὄρη to Trapezus, marking (a) the positions of the Taochi, Chalybes, Scythini, Macrones; (b) the courses of the rivers Teleboas, Centrites, Harpasus. (1873).

1367. Describe the position of Stymphalus, Pisidae, Sicyon, Carduchi, Elis; and draw a rough Map of the return of the Greeks, so far as it is described in Anab. iii. Why did they not return by the road by which they had come? (1886).

1368. Sketch a Map to show the route of the Greeks while passing the Tigris, Euphrates, and their tributaries. (1883).

1369. Describe the nature of the country on the south side of the Euxine, adjoining the coast, pointing out the position of the mountain ranges and principal rivers. (1882).

1370. Describe, or draw a Map of, Media, showing its position in relation to Assyria and Armenia, and marking the sites of Susa and Ecbatana. (1876).

1371. Draw a Map, giving a general idea of the relative positions of Media, Mesopotamia, Armenia, the Persian Gulf, and the Caspian Sea. (1871).

1372. Describe the positions of Sardis, Chaldaea, and Babylonia, and distinguish Syria and Assyria, and Greater and Lesser Phrygia. (1881).

1373. What are the relative positions of Hyrcania and Media to the Persian Gulf and the Caspian Sea? (1881).

1374. Into what sea, and in what direction, does the river Araxes flow? (1876).

1375. Trace roughly the course and direction of the Tigris and the Euphrates, marking the sites of Babylon, Cunaxa, the Carduchi, and Nineveh. In what range of mountains do these rivers take their rise? (1876).

1376. Describe (or show in an outline Map) the sites of Sinope, Heraclea, Lampsacus, Cyzicus, Paphlagonia, and the rivers Halys and Thermodon. (1876).

1377. Name the sites of Susa, Ecbatana, Babylon, Ctesiphon. (1879).

1378. Describe the site of Phoenicia, and of Tyre and Sidon. Write, in brief, what you know of the relation between these cities, and the reasons of their celebrity in antiquity. (1877).

1379. Describe the positions of Sestos, Abydos,

Perinthos, Selybria, Chalcedon, and the Arginusae. (1877).

1380. Describe the sites of Sestus, Halicarnassus, Ephesus, and Sardis, and the rivers Maeander and Pactolus, stating in what respect any of these were specially celebrated. Mark, in outline, the position of Lycia and Caria. (1880).

1381. Describe the position of Pisidia and Cilicia. What mountain-chain bounds the latter on the north, in what direction does it trend, what are its limits further east, and of what rivers is it the watershed ? (1879).

1382. Give the exact position of the following :— Smyrna, Sestus, Epidamnus, Aegina. (1856).

1383. Give the modern names and geographical positions of Anactorium, Naupactus, Rhodos, Chios, Miletus. (1872).

1384. What country is meant by Haemonia? Explain clearly the position of Cenchreae, Mesembria, Tomi, the Symplegades. (1886).

1385. What was the position of the Carduchian mountains, Tigranocerta, the Colchians, Trapezus, Acarnania, Arcadia ? (1883).

1386. Where were Μηονίη ἐρατεινή, Κνωσός, Ὄλυμπος ? (1882).

1387. Define the positions of Calpe, Chrysopolis, Mitylene, Tempe, Pindus and Haemus. (1882).

1388. State what you know of Ephyra, Lycia, the Xanthus, the Solymi, Sidon, the Scaean gate. (1883).

1389. Describe the sites of Chalcedon, Sellasia, Eleusis, Phyle. (1885).

1390. What was the position of Paphos, Argos, Mycenae, Phthia, mount Cynthus, the Carpathian Sea ? (1885).

APPENDIX.

QUESTIONS SET AT THE JUNE EXAMINATION, 1886.

A.—I.

139*a*. State what you know of the Scottish and Irish rebellions under Charles I., and their effect upon the Civil War.

158*a*. Name the members of the Cabal Ministry, and state what led to its fall.

169*a*. William III. acted as his own Foreign Minister. Explain and illustrate this.

178*a*. Give an account of the relations between England and Scotland from the accession of Edward I. to the Battle of Bannockburn.

II.

213*a*. Examine the claims of Stephen and of Matilda to the throne, and describe the effect of their struggle upon the condition of the country.

III.

279*a*. Describe the struggle between John and the Barons, and show how its progress was affected by the relations between John and the King of France.

IV.

418*a*. What do you understand by the parties of the Old and New Learning in the earlier part of the sixteenth century? Name some of the leading adherents of each.

V.

437*a*. Explain the following terms :—Eorl, Ealdorman, Thegn, Reeve, Folkland.

VII.

506*a*. Give a short account of the Danish invasions in the ninth and tenth centuries, and state where the chief Danish settlements were made.

VIII.

594*a*. Describe the career of the Protector Somerset from the death of Henry VIII. to his own fall.

616*a*. State what you know of any four of the following:—Penda, Cuthbert, Caedmon, Bede, Athelstan, Offa, Dunstan.

641*a*. Say what you know of Bishop Burnet, Sir William Temple, John Locke, Algernon Sydney, the first Earl of Shaftesbury, the Duke of Schomberg, General Sarsfield, and the part played by each in the public affairs of their time.

B.

822*a*. Describe the functions of the Praetors at Rome during the Second Punic War.

843*a*. Explain the constitution of a Roman Legion in the time of the elder Scipio.

C.

(No Questions set).

D.

1066*a*. Draw a Map of the Mediterranean Sea, showing the situation of the countries which it touches, and marking the position of the islands. Name the Power to which each of these islands is subject.

K 2

1092a. What are the chief centres of the coal, iron, and cotton industries of England ? Give any circumstances which account for the development of each.

1135a. State the chief directions of English Coonial enterprise during the present century.

1142a. Name the Provinces of Ireland, stating the chief towns in each, and the approximate population of each town.

1196a. Draw a Map of either Yorkshire, Lancashire, or Aberdeenshire, showing the principal towns and rivers in each, and the counties by which it is bordered.

1203a. Compare the extent of sea-board in Britain, France, Germany, and Italy respectively.

E.

1289a. Explain the position of Tarraco, Allifae, Casilinum, Cortona, Arpi, Caere, Antium, Ebusa, Paestum, Ostia.

F.

(No questions set).